THE LANGUAGE OF THE TEENAGE REVOLUTION

THE LANGUAGE OF THE TEENAGE REVOLUTION

The Dictionary Defeated

Kenneth Hudson

First published 1983 by
THE MACMILLAN PRESS LTD
London and Basingstoke
Companies and representatives
throughout the world

ISBN 0 333 29400 9

Printed in Hong Kong

Contents

Acknowledgements

I should like to express my gratitude to the many friends on both sides of the Atlantic and of all ages with whom I have discussed the theme and subject-matter of this book during the past ten years. A number of them are the authors of books and articles mentioned in the sources section at the end of the book and I hope they will forgive me for not repeating their names here.

My very special thanks, however, are due to Helen Martin, who introduced me to invaluable people whom I should never have come across unaided and who carried out much of the time-consuming periodical research which provided me with a considerable proportion of the evidence I needed. I should like to thank, too, the Director and Librarian of Brighton Polytechnic for making their unrivalled collection of material from the underground press available to me. If I had had to rely on the resources of the major libraries for my information, I should have missed a great deal.

K. H.

CHAPTER ONE
What Revolution?[1]

'Between the years 1940 and about 1947', wrote Peter Laslett some twenty years ago,[2] 'I believe there was a critical event in English social development.' This, he believed, was nothing less than a change in the shape of society, a sudden crystallisation of a process which had been gradually developing for generations and which he defined in this way. 'The social height, so to speak, was markedly reduced. From being a pyramid, lofty and slender, society began to look something more like a pear, a pear tending to become an apple. Because it had an altered shape, people began to think about English society differently. Englishmen, perhaps even more Englishwomen, ceased to look upwards as much as they had always done – in short, outward looking began to replace upward looking.'

This is another way of saying that the traditional respect for rank and authority disappeared during the Second World War and the years immediately following it, that the magical prestige of the upper classes was shattered and that Jack no longer had any fear of saying, loudly and in public, that he was as good as his master. The opinion of his peers, not of his superiors, was what mattered. The social gradations of English society no longer interested him and, with money in his pocket and the threat of unemployment removed, he could reasonably feel that the Age of the Common Man had arrived. For the first time he could afford to please himself as to what he did or said, and to show no defer-ence at all either to employers or to dukes.

This change in the shape of English society, to use Laslett's excellent phrase, certainly amounted to a revolution, however many years it may have taken to become fully formed, but it was paralleled by a similar weakening of the previously accepted relationships between the generations. By the 1950s in Britain, and considerably earlier in America, the Teenage Movement had arrived, with its insistence that adolescents should be regarded as a force in their own right, entitled to make their own rules and observe their own standards, without interference from the adult world. Adolescents had become what they had never been before, a sub-culture. It is too convenient and too superficial to say that the new sub-culture was created by powerful commercial interests, who saw a heaven-sent opportunity to create a new and rewarding market for their products, although this was certainly one of the many factors which brought about the revolution and which helped it to establish a recognisable identity.

Equally important was the change in the demographic balance of the nation. Because of the decrease in infant mortality and a spectacular rise in the birthrate, which peaked in 1947, there was, between the mid-1950s and mid-1960s, a doubling of the number of people arriving at the age of 18 each year. There were simply a great many more teenagers about, a fact which made them not only more noticeable, but also more commercially attractive.[3]

One also has to take account of the weakening of the links between parents and children brought about by more widely available educational opportunities and by the need to acquire completely new skills in order to earn a living. In many cases the parents were trained for jobs which are ceasing to exist, so that, not only have they no accumulated knowledge and wisdom to pass on to their children in a way which was previously normal, but they are unable to understand, let alone teach, the standards and values of a social order that has changed radically since they were young. There is a gulf between the generations which has been caused by changing technology.

Moreover, since education, for many boys and girls, now takes much longer than it used to, they spend the whole of their adolescence at close quarters with members of their own age-group, and the results of this can be profound.

'They come to constitute a small society, one that has most of its important interactions within itself, and maintains only a few threads of connexion with the outside adult society. In our modern world of mass communication and rapid diffusion of ideas and knowledge, it is hard to realise that separate sub-cultures can exist right under the noses of adults – sub-cultures with languages all their own, with special symbols, and, most importantly, with value systems that may differ from those of adults. Any parent who has tried to talk to his adolescent son or daughter recently knows this, as does anyone who has recently visited a high school for the first time since his own adolescence. To put it simply, these people speak a different language. What is more relevant to the present point, the language they speak is becoming more and more different.'[4]

Coleman is referring here to boys and girls who remain at school until 18 and who then, in many cases, continue their education at college and university. But the self-contained peer-group, reinforcing the values of its members and conditioning the direction and interests of their lives, has an equally powerful influence at lower social and educational levels. Few, if any, of the parents of Hell's Angels would probably have much understanding of their offspring's code of behaviour, or much sympathy with it, but, for the Angels themselves, membership of the group has been a key factor in their lives, providing mutual sanction and support for a style which would be difficult for an individual to sustain on his own. "The male peer group', decided Peter Wilmott, after a close study of the street gangs of Bethnal Green, 'is a crucial social unit in the lives of the adolescent boys'[5] and, in this respect, there is nothing peculiar or exceptional about East London.

Everyone, perhaps unfortunately, has to spend six years of his or her[6] life as what is now called a teenager, but by no means everyone within this age-group should be identified with the teenage stereotype, which is of someone who is working-class, barely literate, unqualified and disaffected. Teenagers are as varied in their tastes and habits as adults. Some are gentle and some are violent, some work hard at school and some resist all attempts to educate them, some drift regularly in and out of court and some are never in the slightest trouble with the police. Some think of little but pop music and others detest it. As a generalisation 'teenagers' needs to be treated with as much circumspection and suspicion as 'the rich' or 'trade unionists'.

Laslett's pear or apple corresponds as closely to reality as any single metaphor can. The British people as a whole certainly do respect established authority much less than they did fifty or a hundred years ago, especially when what looks and sounds like power and orthodoxy is linked to a title or an office. Compared with their grandparents, they find a much smaller amount of comfort, assurance and guidance coming from above and, in a country where tradition has been a feature of the national life for so long, that constitutes something akin to a revolution. But he would indeed be a bold person who said that the transformation of the pyramid into a pear meant that social aspirations and snobberies were dead in Britain. They may take different forms nowadays, they may possibly be more subtle and less easy for outsiders to recognise. But that they still exist is a fact hardly worth discussion.

As a laboratory of sub-cultures England is unbeatable, yet the wonderful richness and subtlety of the material available to us for study and enjoyment habitually has the life and usefulness squeezed out of it by such crude categorisations as 'the working class', 'teenagers', 'blacks' or 'the stockbroker belt'.

Consider, for instance, three leading members of the British Conservative Party in 1982: Margaret Thatcher, Edward Heath and William Whitelaw, a Prime Minister, an ex-Prime Minister and a Home Secretary. They could all, if one were content to think in these terms, be filed away in drawers labelled 'rich' or 'ruling class' or 'Tories' or 'reactionaries' or 'capitalists' or 'elitists' or whatever other term might come most easily to their political enemies. But to do this would be as ludicrously oversimplified as to lump Arthur Scargill and Tony Benn together as 'left-wing', Sir Colin Davis and Paul McCartney as 'musicians', or Lord Olivier and Sir Harry Secombe as 'actors'. These fundamentally different people appear alike only if they are looked at from a great distance or without one's glasses, so that the significant details cannot be observed, or if one has some special reason, not necessarily sinister, for needing to emphasise similarities rather than differences. On their passports, Lord Olivier and Sir Harry Secombe may both be described as 'actor', without the slightest offence being intended to either. The Passport Office is not in the least interested in what kind of actor one or the other may be or how talented. So far as this particular government department is concerned, these two members of the profession belong to the theatrical sub-culture. That is where they earn their living and their titles.

It would be of considerable interest to know how the great and famous do in fact describe themselves on their passports. Are all footballers 'footballer', all singers 'singer' and all politicians 'politician' and, if not, what are they? Mr Heath would presumably be entitled to call himself 'yachtsman' or 'organist' if he should feel so inclined, but it is unlikely that his passport labels him as either of these.

A person's social group, his sub-culture, is not, of course, wholly determined by his occupation, important a factor as this may be. A more relevant criterion might well be, 'With what kind of people does he tend to pass his time when he is not working?' A tea merchant with a passion for roulette or horse racing is not at all the same kind of person as a tea merchant who devotes his spare time to music or to the study of Chinese. As human beings, rather than as businessmen, they belong to different sub-cultures, understand life in a different way, follow a different set of values.

But one cannot simply say that tea merchant A belongs to a gambling or horsey sub-culture and tea merchant B to a musical or scholarly one and leave it at that. The situation is much more complicated, because in both cases their total way of life includes the things they have in common as well as the things over which they differ. Careful observation of the total pattern of their lives might lead us to several possible conclusions.

1. The two men, as individuals, each belong to more than one sub-culture.
2. Their gambling or music, or whatever their private passion or eccentricity may be, is relatively unimportant by comparison with their other activities.
3. They subscribe to the key values of the social group to which they and, even more important, their wives belong. Their hobbies do not make them heretics. Their homes, their cars, their holidays, the education they choose for their children, their political opinions, their incomes are the determining factors in deciding their sub-culture.

What one does not do is probably quite as crucial as what one does. The people who refrain from hitting their children or their wives as a matter of habit and policy, those whose diet does not include large quantities of potato crisps, those who do not drink large quantities of beer, those who do not shout at their family and acquaintances as a substitute for conversation and discussion belong to a broad, but distinct, sub-culture which the changing shape of English society does not seem to have weakened.

In England, one of the most significant clues to the sub-culture to which one belongs is the way one speaks, especially one's accent and intonation. To appreciate the differnece between Mrs Thatcher, Mr Heath and Mr Whitelaw in this respect demands a good ear and a long experience of the subtleties and idiocies of English society. It is something not easily sensed by a foreigner. One might express the difference by saying that Mr Whitelaw's English is pure white and that of Mrs Thatcher and Mr Heath off-white. Mr Whitelaw speaks the English of the atmosphere in which he was reared as a child, with the unmistakable tune and accent of the British upper class. Mrs Thatcher and Mr Heath, on the other hand, do not speak the English of their childhood; consciously or unconsciously, they have changed their sounds since they became adult. The change has probably been gradual, but in neither case has it reached perfection. It is nearly right, but not quite. To anyone who understands England, it announces as clearly and unmistakably as a biography could that neither Prime Minister was born to the purple. They are, so to speak, self-made.

He would be a bold man who said that Mrs Thatcher and Mr Heath belonged to the same sub-culture. There are very significant differences of background, philosophy, habits and taste. Yet our long-distance observer would almost certainly see them as possessing the essential characteristics of the same breed. They are anti-socialist, they have a considerable amount of money, they are fully literate, they live comfortably, they are accustomed to power, they have no problems in making immediate contact with influential people. Nothing about them suggests the world and outlook of the West Indian carpenter, the office cleaner or the bookmaker.

There are three main causes of confusion, misunderstanding and injustice in the matter of social and cultural labelling. They arise from one's intentions, from the inevitably different results which follow from analysing a group from the inside and from the outside, and from an unwillingness to consider people as individuals rather than members of a class.

As an illustration we could take the techniques employed by the organisers of a trade union or a professional organisation. Here the primary need is to emphasise the solidarity and homogeneous nature of the membership, in order to present the outside world with an image of solid, unbreakable force. Doctors and lorry drivers, for example, are, in each case, as mixed a body of people as one would find anywhere. Their social background is remarkably varied and they have their fair ration of the idle, incompetent and greedy. Yet, whether their trade organisation happens to be the British Medical Association or the Transport and General Workers' Union, they are always offered to the public as a monolithic body of paragons, immensely and consistently hard-working and wholly devoted to the service of the public. The fact that this is a fiction is a matter of common observation but, for professional purposes, there has to be a tightly-knit group labelled 'doctors' or 'lorry drivers', with its distinctive culture and image. Such inconvenient facts as that many lorry drivers on long-distance international runs now have university degrees and that more than a sprinkling of doctors in general practice have the greatest contempt for their fashionable Harley Street colleagues are rigorously suppressed in the never-ending pursuit of unity and group power. The union structure can tolerate neither cracks nor windows pointing in the wrong direction, so the lorry driver with good French or German does not officially exist. Unofficially, however, there is as big a difference between the man shifting containers day after day between Birmingham and Southampton and his colleague mentioned above as between the general practitioner in Bradford and the consultant in Harley Street. Their life-style, their temperament, their associates and their ambitions are a long way apart. To any objective observer – and neither the BMA nor the TGWU can afford to be objective in these matters, or so they believe – they belong to different sub-cultures. And yet it would be absurd to deny that all doctors, like all lorry drivers, have a certain set of skills and interests in common. To that extent, and only to that extent, they are an homogeneous group.

The compulsion which social scientists feel to classify and systematise produces results which require to be interpreted with the greatest caution. Because they are individuals, human beings are all too likely to make a nonsense of any but the most superficial classifications.

That people of all ages do tend to form themselves into rough and ready social groups is undoubtedly true, but these groups are so fluid and their boundaries so untidy that any description of them can properly be no more than tentative and suggestive. What really matters is not the framework, the apparatus and the terminology which allows an academic analyst to construct and formulate his theories about this or that group in society, but what the individual members of the group think about themselves, what models of behaviour they try to follow, what protective colouring they choose to adopt, why they accept the values and characteristics of one group and reject those of another.

A good illustration of the wisdom of allowing people to categorise themselves occurred recently in a perceptive article by Graham Turner about Cheltenham Ladies College, a school frequently attacked, like Eton, as being full of élitist snobs. Such a judgement, Turner discovered, is not at all in accordance with today's facts, whatever the situation may have been a generation ago. New teachers at the school confessed to him that they had been similarly surprised. 'I thought', said the head of the English department, 'they'd be frightfully toffee-nosed, with upper-crust accents, but what I found was quiet, gentle-voiced girls who don't speak as if they've just come off the hunting field, though their mothers sometimes do.'[7] Their fathers tend to be accountants, dentists and company directors rather than peers of the realm, and fewer than half of them have parents who went to boarding schools themselves. Girls who arrive with a 'rah-rah' accent are teased into toning it down. 'The thing is', said one of them, 'we don't want to stick out'. Another explained the new Ladies College outlook in more positive terms. 'It's a form of inverse snobbery', she believed. 'It's considered vulgar now to speak with either an upper- or lower-class accent. If you can achieve a smooth mediocrity, it marks you out as having been to public school.'

Graham Turner defines the new fashionable accent as 'lightly-baked upper-crust à la Rippon'[8] and that is exactly what it is, not Whitelaw, which is too well-baked, nor Thatcher nor Heath, which have been acquired too late to be either smooth or confident. The well-bred person of any generation must never give the appearance of trying. Mrs Thatcher and Mr Heath, on the other hand, are not completely at ease with their accents. Like Mr Roy Jenkins, they try just a little too hard.

The young ladies at Cheltenham have a fairly clear idea of what they ought to be doing in order to achieve the difficult feat of discreetly maintaining their status and that of their families and at the same time protecting themselves as best they can against the attacks of a society which is becoming increasingly critical of the moneyed class to which they belong and of highly privileged schools like the Ladies College. A 'smooth mediocrity' seems, in all the circumstances, to be a very sensible armour to wear.

But what, in that case, is one to do about the U and non-U labels, so treasured by observers of the English social and linguistic scene since Professor Alan Ross first offered them to the world in 1954?[9] Vital as they may have been to the parents and grandparents of the girls now at Cheltenham, how important are they still to the new generation, or to their male equivalents at Eton, Winchester and elsewhere?

Professor Ross recognised that the situation was changing all the time. Nothing, he admitted in his 1968 follow-up article,[10] could be considered permanent, but certain peculiarities of upper-class speech appeared to have more stamina than others. 'Home', he felt, was a good example. Writing in the late 1960s, he believed that "They've a lovely home' was as non-U as it had ever been and I think it is extremely likely that today's 18-year-olds at Cheltenham would agree with him. As a joke it would be possible for them to use, but they would feel that one would have to be very lower-middle-class to use such an expression without having one's tongue in one's cheek, and so, too, with most of the other words and phrases which were being confidently ticketed non-U by Professor Ross at about the time when Graham Turner's interviewees were learning to read – cocktails, half-ten, handbag, phone, raincoat, that's right, settee, couch, titled, suite, starter and all the rest of the off-white vocabulary.

One has to be careful not to say that such words are shunned by these girls and boys. They are, in fact, used quite often, but in inverted commas, with a faint touch of mockery in the voice. This habit of making fun of the expressions favoured by other social classes and previous generations is very widespread among young people nowadays. It is discussed at length in Chapter 5, under the heading 'Wrong-footing the Enemy', and it represents a profound difference between the linguistic psychology of today and fifty years ago, an effective and subtle way of hunting with both the hare and the hounds. It is one of the most important reasons why the preparation of satisfactory dictionaries of modern English is almost impossible. So many words and phrases are used both straight and ironically, and one has to know where a person places himself in society, what his philosophy is and where his allegiances lie in order to decide how he is likely to be using a particular word. One never knows who or what the next victim of a linguistic take-over is going to be, who is going to be mocked or crucified by the all-powerful inverted commas. Consider, for example, this paragraph from Alan Ross's reassessment of U speech.

> Forty years ago, male acquaintances (of many classes, includ-ing the U) called each other by the basic surname. Between males the use of Christian names indicated a considerable degree of intimacy, and, between male and female, at least a moderate degree. Now the use of Christian names – between the most diverse persons – is almost universal. It appears, too, that a non-U Mr Smith is definitely insulted if he is called Smith. Further, in talking about him, John Smith is always called John Smith (not Mr Smith).

To say this is, of course, to overlook organisations, like prisons and the armed forces, which operate under a strict system of discipline and where those at the receiving end of the discipline are always referred to by only their surnames. But, in general, what Ross says is perfectly correct. The Holmes-and-Watson form of address has virtually disappeared from civilian life, for the moment. I would not be at all surprised, however, to see it return as a new fashion among the young. The Christian name fetish may already be in the process of losing its attraction and, in an age of violence and toughness, the crude, abrupt surname would have much to commend it, especially if it were used ironically, as it might well be. The time may be ripe for its introduction: the all-pervading Christian name could be acquiring a certain flavour of softness, even when it is shortened to give it an extra democratic edge. The days of Mike Jones, Director of Social Services for Ruffletown, and Steve Smith, Bishop of Widnes, may be drawing to an end. Ten years from now the pupils of Cheltenham Ladies College could well be saying 'Mike Jones' in inverted commas, just as they gently smile their way through 'a beautiful home' today.

To do this is something quite different from rejecting the ideas and habits of one's parents. It is a way of cutting older people down to size, of digesting and regurgitating their beliefs and customs in a way which makes clear that what is being recycled is merely a selection of all the possibilities, reproduced in a slightly caricatured form, so that there can be no question of who is in control of the situation. It is essentially a group activity, carried out in the knowledge that other members of the group will recognise and understand the code, a mark of confidence and poise, rather than of protest.

The mind of the true rebel, the individualist who decides to cut his roots, works differently. The writer and broadcaster Ray Gosling is a good example.[11] Born in 1939 in Northampton, his mother was an infant teacher and came from a family of farm workers. His father 'mended motor bikes and then motor cars' and was self-educated. He himself went to the local grammar school, which his parents saw as the foundation of all their hopes for him, but perversely he turned his back on it. He tells us:

> Already at fifteen I knew that I had rejected one by one the opportunities they saved up to provide me with, and I was rejecting little by little the way of life that would give me a happy and secure and better future, and for them the sense of satisfaction and success. I was throwing dirt on home and myself.[12]

He rebelled in nearly every way that was open to him. His parents paid for elocution lessons, but he abandoned them 'and cultivated, to their disappointment, the accents of the scruffy and the secondary modern schoolchildren. I liked the common language.' He had piano and violin lessons, 'but these I decided I didn't want. I wanted the radio, the juke box and the hurdy gurdy of the hooligan.'

He was determined to stay at the bottom of the pile, and to oppose any attempt to turn him into a future member of the middle class. When he was in the sixth form he helped to keep himself by working in the holidays as a railway signalman. At the same time, as a further assertion of his independence and individuality, he became a Catholic. He did other odd jobs while he was at school and then, having decided to drop out of education, he left home and went to live in Liverpool and Leicester, supporting himself by doing unskilled factory work. After that, he tried the University of Leicester for a year, but found it impossible to get on with his fellow students. 'The one thing that got me', he recalls, 'was the total lack of curiosity, the complete deadness of any imagination or awareness. Their interest stopped at the syllabus and the social round.'

With the university safely out of the way, he started a revolutionary youth club, which folded, and then moved over to journalism and broadcasting, in which he has made a successful career.

Ray Gosling is an untypical member of his generation, not because he rejected the conventional opportunities which were offered to him, but because he has written and published an analysis of his motives and behaviour. He has taken great pains to present himself to us as an individual, not as a symbol of a revolution. We are not invited to see him as an awkward adolescent, and Angry Young Man of the 1960s, as a university dropout, as a hater of middle-class values, as anything or anybody other than himself. There may or may not be thousands like him; it is a point he does not ask us to consider.

But, even so, the decisions he took cannot have been entirely unaffected by the social and political atmosphere of the 1950s, the decade of his teenage. He was 12 at the time of the Festival of Britain and the fall of the Labour Government, 14 when Stalin died, 16 when commercial television arrived, Mary Quant opened her Bazaar in the King's Road and *Waiting for Godot* was produced at the Arts Theatre, and 17 when Colin Wilson's *The Outsider* appeared and the Royal Court put on John Osborne's *Look Back in Anger*, with its message that the upper middle class was finished and that the future belonged to Jimmy Porter and to those like him, young, working-class, aggressive and the articulate enemies of good taste. It was a good time to be a rebel. One was surrounded by people who looked and sounded like allies and the air was full of seductive movements which one was flattered to join.

Professor Brian Morris wrote years afterwards:

It is entirely characteristic that, though no heads rolled, no blood was spilt and no bastion fell, the events which took place in London in the years following 1955 should be immediately dignified with the name of 'Revolution' . . . In 1967 the *Guardian* could announce, 'The revolution is over', and prophesy 'a period of consolidation'. The word used to describe the death of Charles I, the fall of the Bastille, the rise of Marxism–Leninism in Russia, was flashed across the media to encapsulate the coming of Carnaby Street, the disputes at the London School of Economics, Supermac, CND, the Beatles and the mini-skirt.[13]

Movements and revolutions are raw material for the sociologist and historian to process, but to concentrate on individuals is the privilege of the artist. The scientist, of whatever type, is concerned with what he has reason to believe are the common qualities of large numbers of individuals, with classes and with classification. His work and theories are based on general concepts, on material capable of statistical analysis. In the social science field, we therefore have strangely unreal creatures called 'young affluents', 'working-class parents', the 'middle-class mother', people without names and faces, people without problems, talents and opportunities peculiar to themselves.

Consider two talks broadcast by the BBC in 1963 – when, in the *Guardian's* view, the revolution was drawing to an end – and subsequently reprinted. The first, by Dennis Chapman, was called 'The Autonomous Generation' and the second, by Alan Little, 'The Young Affluents'. Both are about people-as-members-of-categories, not about the individuals one actually meets, and both make judgements which could certainly be repeatedly challenged, if one had the time and the energy to test each generalisation against a hundred or a thousand real people. 'X', we should then say, 'isn't like this at all', or 'Yes, Y is something like that, but he does this or thinks that as well, and that changes the picture completely'. It may suit the farmer's way of running his business to pretend that all his cows are identical, but his herdsman knows better.

When any group in society fails to understand another [pontificates Mr Chapman] it responds in the most primitive way. It threatens, attacks, finds faults, blames and reproaches. So it is with many adults faced with the present generation of young people, a generation largely independent of, and isolated from their elders. It is this separation of the generations which makes the behaviour of the young so puzzling to us. They are rejecting the values of adult society and have adopted for themselves a romantic puritanism. Their mentors are teachers, philosophers and theologians, and the 'pop' singers who offer the promise of love. If we look closely, we shall find behind this an important

social change. Health, economic independence, and education
have made it possible for a generation, perhaps for the first
time in history, to choose for themselves an ethic by which to
live.[14]

Mr Little sees the young in much the same way. In the past, he
tells us, there has been a great deal of publicity for untypical
adolescents – street arabs, delinquents, teddy boys – but the
emphasis has now shifted from the untypical to the typical. In his
opinion,

> what is new is that the recent attention is not confined to the
> majority of the age group, but is being given either to the bulk
> of the teenage population, or to a dominant minority whose
> attitude and behaviour serve as an example to the rest. Who
> are these 'typical' or dominant affluents? To me, they are the
> young affluents. George Melly, the jazz singer and journalist,
> suggests that they are 'not strictly anyone between the age of
> thirteen and twenty, but a moneyed group between those ages
> who are able to afford what they want and decide their own
> pattern of life, which is very different from their parents. They
> come from the upper working and lower middle class.[15]

It all sounds very plausible and it confirms many of one's own
impressions and prejudices, but is it true? In 1963 Britain was
suffering from delayed shock and excitement about something
that was being called, somewhat rashly perhaps, the Teenage
Revolution, and journalists, television producers and sociologists
were busy discovering that there were interesting differences
between the adolescents of the 1930s on the one hand and those of
the 1950s and 1960s on the other. By the end of the decade, however, some observers at least had begun to wonder if the new
generation was quite as remarkable and all of a piece as it was
made out to be. In a refreshing article, bearing the title 'Non-
Swinging Youth',[16] Bernard Davies pointed out that there was
plenty of evidence that 'everything that is young does not swing'.
His researches in the northern industrial districts had revealed a
great slice of working-class boys and girls who were neither big
spenders nor stylish dressers, and who seemed to him to have
much the same sort of problems and aspirations as their parents
at the same age, although a number of them made a rather sad

attempt to acquire a swinging veneer for the brief period before the cares and responsibilities of adulthood finally descended upon them. What, Bernard Davies very sensibly asked, are the real boundaries of this thing we have been calling 'youth culture'? How many sub-species is it allowed to have before it ceases to have any validity or usefulness as a 'culture'?

There is, of course, a great deal of truth and insight in Chapman's concept of 'the autonomous generation', and Little's of 'the young affluents'. Compared with their parents and grand-parents, boys and girls in the 1960s were, on the whole, able to lead more independent lives and to do things which would previously been impossible for most people in this age-group. No doubt the teenagers of the 1970s considered their predecessors of the 1960s to have been quaintly old-fashioned in many ways and without advantages which they themselves had. It is equally possible that those who are 16 and 18 today often marvel at the low prices of ten years ago and at the ease with which jobs and money were available. We may soon find them being described as 'the deprived generation' or something equally over-generalised and newsworthy.

But, in every decade, what we really have to consider, assuming that we are concerned with reality, not journalistic or academic fiction, is what individual people, of all ages, think about society and their place in it. What do they want to do, whom do they see as their allies and enemies, what kind of social groupings and distinguishing characteristics make them feel happier, more confident and more secure? To explore the answers to these questions is to become aware that, whatever may have been the case in prehistoric or medieval times, our society today is made up, not of classes, but of a multitude of subtly different sub-cultures which overlap at many points and some-times coalesce temporarily in order to meet a particular threat or opportunity. Everyone is aware, in a vague way, of the sub-culture or sub-cultures to which he or she belongs and everyone resents, often bitterly and violently, any attempt from outside to place him in a social category to which he knows he does not belong.

Many people have no business to exist, because they refuse to fit the categories the sociologists have provided for them. One can easily think of examples: the teenagers who hate discos; quiet, studious blacks; people in bed-sitters who do not read the

Guardian; art students who favour representational art and can draw; doctors and dentists who have never owned a boat; contented farmers. This is not to say that the whole notion of sub-cultures is a myth, merely a warning that the interrelation of cultures, sub-cultures and sub-sub-cultures is exceedingly complex, often to the point of defying analysis and classification. The revolution has taken place and life will never be the same again, but many people have apparently been content to let it roll over them and to follow their own interests and to cultivate their own intellectual and emotional garden. In later years, to the question, 'What did you do in the Great Revolution, daddy?', they are very likely to ask, 'What Revolution?'

CHAPTER TWO
Attitudes to Words

One of the best-known and most influential sociolinguists of the post-war period is Professor Basil Bernstein, of the Institute of Education at the University of London. Bernstein set out to discover why some children succeeded at school and others failed. His conclusion was that schools were geared to the habits and attitudes of what he decided, for reasons of convenience, to call the middle class, and that working-class children – another label of convenience – were consequently disadvantaged from the beginning of their school careers.

A formidable structure of influential linguistic theory has grown from this decision to divide society – or rather, British society – into these two cultural halves. The theory could be explained roughly as follows. 'One of the aims of the middle class family', says Bernstein, 'is to produce a child oriented to certain values but individually differentiated within them. The child is born into an environment where he is seen and responded to as an individual with his own rights, that is, he has specific social status.'[1] The parents watch the child carefully and encourage him to use words in a way which will express his feelings about the world around him, to become 'sensitive to a particular form of indirect or mediate expression where the subtle arrangement of words and connexions between sentences conveys feeling'.[2] An emphasis is placed on the 'verbalization of feeling'. 'The language-use of the middle-class', Bernstein believes, 'is rich in personal, individual qualifications, and its form implies sets of advanced logical operations; volume and tone and other non-verbal means of expression, although important, take second place.'[3] The middle-class child at an early age becomes sensitive to a complex form of language use which determines the way in which he regards objects and which gives him a skill and confidence in manipulating words. For him, school continues and enhances these attitudes.

Working-class language psychology, in Bernstein's view, is quite different. It is based on a form of language which he calls 'public', in contra-distinction to middle-class language, which is 'formal'. 'If the words used are part of a language which contains a high proportion of short commands, simple statements and questions where the symbolism is descriptive, tangible, concrete, visual and of a low order of generality, where the emphasis is on the emotive rather than the logical implications, it will be called a *public* language.'[4]

The working-class family has a more authoritarian structure and its aims and expectations are shorter-term. Preferences, goals and dissatisfactions follow a different pattern. 'Present gratifications or present deprivations become absolute gratifications or absolute deprivations, for there exists no developed time continuum upon which present activity can be ranged. Relative to the middle classes, the postponement of present pleasure for future gratifications will be found difficult.'[5] This produces a constant clash between school and the working-class child. The school says, in effect, 'Work hard now and you will have a much better life later on', but the working-class child, like the working-class adult, is not prepared to wait. Any effort which does not yield immediate dividends is not worth making. And there is another important difference between the two. 'The level of curiosity of the working-class child is relatively low, and as compared with the middle-class child, differently oriented, and this removes a powerful stimulus from the classroom. The working-class child has a preference for descriptive cognitive responses; his response is an immediate one and only vague extensions in time and space, and consequently his attention will be brief or difficult to sustain without punitive measures. Rather than pursuing the detailed implications and relations of an object or an idea, which at once create the problem of its structure and extensions, he is oriented towards the cursory examinations of a series of different items.'[6] He sees statements and facts in isolation and finds it difficult to fit them into a pattern.

An individual may have both a public language and a formal language at his disposal, or he may be limited to one, the public language. Whether he has one or two languages will depend on his social group. A middle-class person is likely to have the choice of two; a working-class person will speak and understand only one. Translation between the two is almost impossible, although a rough approximation often has to be attempted by those who, like teachers, find themselves in positions of intermediaries, middle-men between one social class and another. The main cause of this untranslatability is that public language emphasises the supreme importance of social relations and emotions, while formal language gives priority to individual feelings and qualifications, and is rooted in them.

Those whose language is only public are likely either to be forced to express their feelings in ways not related to linguistic skill - shouting, violence, rioting, vandalism - or to suppress or deny feelings, such as guilt or shame, for which they have no words. Bernstein is particularly perceptive on this point. Speaking of public language, he says:

> Tender feelings which are personal and highly individual will not only be difficult to express in this linguistic form, but it is likely that the objects which arouse tender feelings will be given touch terms, particularly those referring to girl friends, love, death and disappointments. The experience of tender feelings, as with any situation which forces the need to produce individual qualifications, may produce feelings of acute embarrassment, discomfort, a desire to leave the field and denial or hostility towards the object which aroused the tender feelings. To speakers of a *public* language, tender feelings are a potential threat, for in this experience is also the experience of isolation - social isolation.[7]

Social and linguistic attitudes are transmitted and strengthened by what Bernstein calls 'codes'. 'Individuals', he says, 'come to learn their social roles through the process of communication. A social role from this point of view is a constellation of shared, learned meanings through which individuals are able to enter stable, consistent and publicly recognised forms of interaction with others. A social role can then be considered as a complex coding activity controlling both the creation and organisation of specific meanings and the conditions for their transmission and reception.'[8]

He distinguishes between 'restricted' and 'elaborated' codes. The restricted code emerges where the culture or sub-culture raises the 'we' above 'I'. It 'creates social solidarity at the cost of individual experience', and functions as both the control and transmitter of the culture in such varied groups as 'prisons, the age-group of adolescents, army, friends of long standing, between husband and wife.'[9]

The elaborated code, on the other hand, will arise wherever the culture or sub-culture emphasises the 'I' over the 'we'. 'It will arise wherever the intent of the other person cannot be taken for granted. In as much as the intent of the other person cannot be taken for granted, then speakers are forced to elaborate their meanings and make them both explicit and specific.'[10] The true and most significant aspect of social and educational privilege, Bernstein points out, is consequently the acquisition of the elaborated code and, conversely, one of the most serious effects of the class system, in Bernstein's view, 'is to limit access to elaborated codes'. Expressed in more traditional terms, the division between the two Englands is nowadays not so much between the rich and the poor as between the users of the elaborated and the users of the restricted code.

But Bernstein's theories, stimulating though they may be, are based on enormous generalisations. Even if one were to arrive at satisfactory definitions of middle class and working class, which is well-nigh impossible, it would be ridiculous to pretend that every family which fell into one or the other category used either the formal or the public language appropriate to it, or was governed by the elaborated or restricted code. There are plenty of quietly spoken, sensitive working-class families, just as there is a distressingly large number of middle-class people whose language is assuredly not 'rich in personal, individual qualifications'. But, as a rough and ready touchstone, Bernstein's theories and those of his disciples make sense and are helpful in hacking one's way through the jungle of modern English usage.

One of the biggest eye- and ear-openers for middle-class people in recent times was a television series called *The Family*, broadcast by the BBC during 1976. The film unit spent many months in a working-class, public-language household in Reading, observing and documenting the family's daily activities and conversations, and the results undoubtedly came as a considerable surprise to the great majority of 'formal' people. What was particularly instructive was the discovery that the two generations of the family – mother, father and grown-up children

- living together in the same house rarely had what the 'formal' viewers would have termed a conversation or discussion. Every exchange of words had the flavour of a quarrel, or of statement meeting counter-statement, or of nagging, attacking someone with the same demand over and over again in the hope of eventually getting one's way by tiring out the other party, a normal feature of what are flatteringly called 'negotiations' between trade unionists and employers. The 'public' performers in the television series and the 'formal' viewers of the programme had much the same words at their disposal, but the method of using them was quite different, and the shock of realising this was not dissimilar to that which a well-to-do Victorian would have experienced when visiting a slum and hearing about the inhabitants' problems and way of life. The social changes of the previous half-century had evidently done very little to break down the barrier between what still appeared to be two different species of humanity.

In observing and analysing this situation, the sociologist is in a difficult position. He is not necessarily saying, 'Here is the middle class and here is the working class. I shall now proceed to discover and describe certain of their characteristics and habits.' What is equally, possibly more, likely to happen is that he will say, in effect, 'Here are two sections of humanity who seem to think and talk about life in a quite different fashion. Since one is largely made up of people who are paid weekly and includes those who do relatively menial work and the other of salary-carners, including many in responsible positions, I shall, for the convenience of setting out my argument, call the first category working class and the second middle class.' The dangers implicit in such an approach are evident, notwithstanding the fact that most of the people in each category may obligingly come fairly close to the stereotype provided for them. But the extent to which people do not fit the stereotype, do not conform to the generalisation, is surely what makes them interesting, significant and important. One cannot very well construct norms, which always involve some degree of distortion of the facts as they really are, and then get angry with those who, for the reason or another, fail to match up to the norms. The person with extra-big feet does unfortunately exist, however much the shoemaker and the shopkeeper may decide to ignore him.

Consider this statement:

Generally, the research has shown that middle-class parents provide more warmth and are more likely to use reasoning, isolation, show of disappointment, or guilt-arousing appeals in disciplining the child. They are also likely to be more permissive about demands for attention from the child, sex behaviour, aggression to parent, table manners, neatness and orderliness, noise, bedtime rules, and general obedience. Working-class parents are more likely to use ridicule, shouting, or physical punishment in disciplining the child, and to be generally more restrictive. [11]

The two key words are 'generally' and 'likely'. The author is describing trends, as he sees them, not laying down rules, and the qualifiers are widely included. The fact that many parents behave in a manner which is untypical of the social class to which they are, by other criteria, judged to belong may be highly regrettable to those who like categories to be tidy round the edges, but nevertheless it corresponds to the untidiness and perversity of life as it is actually lived.

Yet Bernstein's analysis, and indeed the material which it interprets, may already be out of date. A movement supporting and encouraging both non-literacy and anti-literacy has for some years been showing signs of sweeping through all social classes. Its progress by the end of the century may well cause the next generation of social and linguistic scientists to reconsider the conclusions which are so widely accepted at the present time, and with which Bernstein's name is particularly associated.

During the period following the Second World War, there has been a marked fall in the prestige of words, or at least of words handled skilfully. More and more of the information needed by the mass consumer society has been transmitted pictorially, more and more of the thinking and communication of the best paid and most influential group has been carried out by means of mathematical, not verbal, symbols. Numeracy has been replacing literacy. To be fully literate, in the traditional sense, was to be 'caught in the net of the old values', [12] to cut oneself off from the mainstream of contemporary culture. The modern helot is innumerate, not, as before, illiterate. Literature finds itself more and more divorced from the aims and practice of education, and the language of sensitivity and response, the distinguishing feature of Bernstein's middle-class, is battered, undermined and downgraded by the twin assaults of science and money-making pragmatism.

For half a century at least, the humanist and the mass media have been perpetually and implacably at war with each other. The humanist, with his roots in the past, emphasises human differences – his allegiance has to be to formal language – and he urges toleration towards views, tastes and habits which are not our own; the mass media, stressing the super-relevance of the present, depend for their acceptance and prosperity on the concept of the average man, of standardised attitudes and beliefs. They are necessarily wedded to public language, because that is the language of the majority of their customers. Mass culture transforms everything into what Bernard Rosenberg has well called 'the same soft currency'.[13] For the mass media the market cannot be too big, not too homogenous. The culture to which they give their immensely powerful support is based on the creed that everything can and must be made effortless and immediately understandable, a state of affairs which is possible only if that culture is at a very low level. The concept of the teenager is a perfect reflection of this philosophy. It has led to the creation of an artificial stereotype, based on the individual who has left school at the earliest possible age and gone immediately into an unskilled and probably dead-end job, the person who lives only in his free time and for whom all satisfactions must be facile and immediate. 'It is', observes B. Sugarman, 'no accident that the heroes of youth culture – pop singers, song writers, clothes designers and others – have mostly achieved their positions without long years of work or sacrifice.'[14]

But pop music is not only a matter of music. The culture surrounding it and largely created by it has been the major carrier of change during the past thirty years, the magic carpet which has gone from country to country and continent to continent as if national frontiers and iron curtains did not exist. With pop music to sweep them along, new attitudes to drugs, sex, dress, money, education, class and religion have tracked their way across the world at a pace which makes previous international movements of ideas seem elephantine by comparison. In the process pop culture has created a new language, a new attitude to words. To devote our next chapter to this is consequently neither whimsical not self-indulgent. Pop and everything that goes with it is central to a study of what has been happening to the English language in recent years.

Words are, of course, only one type of language and their relative importance to other kinds of language has always been exaggerated by those who earn a living and win social prestige by using words skilfully. What is new about the post-1945 situation is that those who are skilled in handling words are, at least in Britain, no longer regarded with any particular deference by those, the majority, whose vocabulary is small, and whose grammar and syntax are shaky, clumsy and inaccurate. In linguistic matters, as in all others, Jack considers himself to be every bit as good as his master or, rather, he has ceased to acknowledge that he has any masters. Something of the old respect for good writing and careful, precise speaking remains among older people, but it is rare nowadays to find it among the young.

 This change of attitude is reflected in the increasing use of the word 'communication', as a more 'democratic' replacement for the more old-fashioned 'language'. 'If', says Mary Douglas, 'we ask of any form of communication the simple question, "What is being communicated?", the answer is "information from the social system". The exchanges which are being comunicated constitute the social system.'[15] An important feature of the social system within which we in the Western world live is that it is pluralistic. There are many sub-systems meshing into one another and combining to form the total complex which goes by the name of the English Social System. In such circumstances 'communication' is both within a group and between one group and another and the same word, expression, way of eating or form of dressing is likely, if not certain, to have significantly different meanings, to communicate differently, inside and outside the group.

M. A. K. Halliday makes this point very well:

What one group interprets as an occasion for a public declaration of private faith may be seen by the second group as an exchange of observations about the objective world, and by a third group as something else again – as a game, for example. Interaction between the generations, and between the sexes is full of semiotic mismatches of this kind. It is not just the individual as an individual that we identify by his semantic profile; it is the individual as a member of his social group. The city-dweller is remarkable only by the number of different social groups in which he typically holds a membership at any one time. [16]

The situation is complicated, as Halliday points out, by the desire of some people to avoid the possibility of being understood, at least outside the group to which they belong. What they create for themselves is 'anti-language', which one could define as 'the special language of people who choose to be outside society'. [17] The language of these people is secret, because the reality is secret. Those who create it and use it 'are constantly striving to maintain a counter-reality that is under pressure from the established world. This is why the language is constantly renewing itself – to sustain the vitality that it needs if it is to function at all. Such is the most likely explanation of the rapid turnover of words and modes of expression that is always remarked on by commentators on underworld language.' [18]

We are therefore faced with a paradox of 'new' language appearing fresh and lively to society as a whole, but dead and old to those who brought it into being in the first place. Its 'meaning' changes as it moves socially and for this reason any description of it has to be so flexible and so fluid as to burst the banks of a dictionary. We must, in other words, think of language communities, rather than languages. The unit of description has to be social and communication is a matter of much more than mere words. Even if one confines one's attention to what are nowadays known as 'speech communities', one's approach cannot, if one's analysis and interpretation is to make sense and be helpful, be anything other than social. The speech community is 'a community sharing knowledge of rules for the conduct and interpretation of speech', [19] and its 'speech' has to be set firmly and continuously in its total context. 'One starts with a social group and considers the entire organisation of linguistic means within it, rather than start with some one partial, named organisation of linguistic means, called a "language". This is vital, because the notion of "a language" can carry with it a confusion of several notions and attributes that in fact have to be sorted out.' [20]

The pop world – that is, the post-1945 youth culture with pop music as its core – has been consistently prejudiced against the written word and equally consistently in favour of what is spoken or sung. The written word, especially in the form of a book

between hard covers, represents permanence. It suggests a continuum of experience, whereas the essence of pop is that it
concentrates wholly on the present moment. It is interested
neither in the past nor in the future. Writing and reading are bad
from another point of view. They are necessarily solitary
activities. The person who reads is in a private world, inhabited
only by himself and the author. Pop, on the other hand, is
necessarily communal. Its impact and its point depends on
sharing one's experiences with other people. The lonely pop fan
is a contradiction in terms.

Moreover, as George Melly emphasised at the beginning of the
1970s, pop demands 'a deliberate impoverishment of vocabulary'.
Those committed to it, he noted,

> are in many cases literate and educated, but, voluntarily, they
> have reduced their word power to a few basic and nebulous
> expressions. Pop slang, unlike that of earlier closed societies
> such as the jazz world or the underworld, is without colour,
> without vivid or racy metaphor, without room for personal
> improvisation.
>
> It changes, of course. Its sense of exclusivity demands that as
> rock and the media have made its passwords public knowledge
> they must be rejected, but even here it tends to revert back to
> earlier expressions rather than invent or take over new ones
> from other sources. It's more the way in which this basic
> language is put together that counts. It's the rhythm which acts
> as the signal by which one member of the pop society recognises
> another.[21]

Clothing, hair and adornment have become a language, a
method of communication, an indication that like is calling to
like, in a way that hardly existed before the Second World War.
It is difficult to decide whether pop or jeans have been the most
profound and widespread cause of solidarity among the world's
teenagers during the past thirty years. Denim, the jeans material,
had a prosaic enough beginning. Originally used for making
tents, it came into favour during the California gold-rush of the
1850s, when the corners of the pockets were reinforced to stop
them tearing under the strain of carrying ore samples. A hundred
years later, by a stroke of commercial genius, Levi Strauss turned
jeans into an article of teenage clothing that matched the new

classless mood to perfection and made a great fortune for the
manufacturer of these hard-wearing, cheap garments. Partly by
their American associations, partly as a result of extremely skilful
marketing, they became something much more than a covering
for the lower half of the body. They were a language, an assertion
of identity.

Business acumen 'made a simple commercial product somehow
synonymous with freedom, youth, virility, independence and
adventure – all without the massive force-feed advertising typical
of Coca-Cola or Ford. There is an intriguing ambiguousness
about the Levi's mystique. It manages to symbolise not only male
and female sexuality, but the camp restlessness of our time's
high fashion. It implies egalitarianism, working-class values, and
solidarity with the poor, even to becoming the international
uniform of youthful radicalism, yet board chairmen wear them to
meetings, their wives buy them already patched and recycled at
L. Magnim's and the hearty rancher and fruit-grower who are
still fighting the unionisation of their migrant help have been
Levi's people from the beginning.'[22]

Jeans took some time to move up the age-groups. In their best
days, in the 1950s and 1960s 'anytime, anywhere, wearing a pair
of Levi's was like wearing your heart on your sleeve. A pair of
Levi's said younger generation, flexible person, still growing, not
like your parents.'[23]

And, to weaken the power of words still further as a means of
communication, the picture, whether static, as in photographs or
strip cartoons, or moving, as in films and television, has become
increasingly important as a means of communication. It has sub-
divided culture still further, with the fully literate becoming a
small minority. As Marshall McLuhan puts it,

Highly literate people cannot cope with the nonverbal art of
the pictorial, so they dance impatiently up and down to express
a pointless disapproval that renders them futile and gives new
power and authority to the ads. The unconscious depth-
messages of ads are never attacked by the literate, because
of their incapacity to notice or discuss nonverbal forms of
arrangement and meaning. They have not the art to argue
with pictures. When early in TV broadcasting hidden ads were
tried out, the literate were in a great panic until they were
dropped. The fact that typography is itself mainly subliminal

in effect and that pictures are, as well, is a secret that is safe
from the book-oriented community.[24]

Noises have come to take official precedence over words as an
expression of feeling. Unofficially, they have always been more
important, but it has taken pop songs to make the point clear, to
emphasise that sounds matter more than words, that communication does not involve meaning.

After studying rock lyrics more intensively than most people
would want to, Simon Frith came to a firm conclusion. 'Pop
songs', he decided, 'celebrate not the articulate, but the inarti-
culate, and the evaluation of pop singers depends not on words
but on voices, on the voices around the words. This is not at all
surprising. In our daily lives, the most directly intense statements
of our feelings involve not words but noises. We sigh and gasp, we
moan, guffaw, cry, cheer, and so on. We even measure the
intensity, the profundity, the originality of our feelings by
reference to our inability to find immediate words for them.'[25]

There is a good deal to be said for this point of view, but it
appears to overlook the not unimportant matter of sincerity. The
sighs, gasps and moans of pop singers are entirely synthetic. The
singers do not really experience these emotions, emotions which,
we are told, cannot be expressed in words. They do what is
expected of them. The noises they make, the habitual shutting
of the eyes, are entirely ritualistic, which does not, of course,
make them any less powerful in their effect. The point is simply
that sincerity is required of a poet; it is not required of a pop
singer, or of the person who writes what he sings.

Three quite different considerations are involved in discussing
how the products of what we are calling, for convenience, the
Teenage Revolution use and view language. The first is the
general linguistic climate of the age, irrespective of generations or
individuals. The second is any gap in communication or in styles
of communication which may exist between young people and
their parents, any break in tradition. And the third is the relative
importance of words as a means of communication. The three
approaches are, of course, closely interlocked. We can illustrate
this by looking at the recent history of a single key word.

'Harass', in the sense of 'worry' or 'annoy', has been used in
English since the early seventeenth century. It was particularly
common in military circles. One 'harassed the enemy', much as a

wasp annoys a picnic party, by persistent, needling attacks. It belonged, until about ten years ago, to no particular social group or level: it was a neutral, colourless kind of word, little used by most people from one year's end to another. The adjective, 'harassed', was probably heard more often. Mothers of small children frequently and understandably described themselves as 'harassed'. 'A harassed mother' was almost a compound noun.

In the late 1970s 'harassed' and 'harassment' quite suddenly became explosive words. Young people, especially if they happened to be black, decided they were being 'harassed by the police and more recently still, in 1980 and 1981, 'police harassment' has been given by members of the black community in Britain as a principal cause of riots. 'Harassment' is now one of the most emotionally charged and socially divisive words in the language.

It is something of a waste of time to try to define such a loaded term, but one has to make the attempt, knowing that any dictionary-length is bound to be unsatisfactory and that even a short essay cannot deal adequately with the controversy that surrounds this unfortunate word. One could usefully begin by asking a few carefully selected people, some black, some white, and of various ages, to say what they understand by 'harassment'. Two pieces of information are likely to emerge from their answers: first, that everybody's thinking is influenced by the current cliché, 'police harassment', and that few find it possible to consider the word in another context; and, second, that young blacks and young working-class whites are so convinced that they are 'harassed' by the police, singled out for specially prejudiced and vindictive treatment, that they are hardly prepared to consider the matter. A great many, possibly the majority, of their fellow-citizens would probably disagree with them. For one group, therefore, 'harassment' is part of a creed, a badge of group solidarity, a common token of suffering, but to another it is an irritant, an idiocy, something they refuse to believe or take seriously.

What dictionary definition can hope to record or to do justice to such a situation? The best it might achieve could be something like this:

Harassment The act of troubling or annoying by repeated attacks. Since *c.* 1978 used especially in the compound 'police harassment', a concept strenuously denied by the police but fervently believed by most English blacks and by a section of urban working-class young males.

This definition is not of the normal dictionary type, but it is difficult to see how the task could be carried out very differently. Yet even a long and discursive entry like this can give only an approximate idea of the social framework within which the words 'harass' and 'harassment' are used, of their cultural overtones. For a full awareness of their contexts, not only must one live, move about and listen in the society which makes use of such expressions, but one must do so over a much wider spectrum than most people would find either possible or agreeable.

The average person has a range of acquaintances and contacts which is extremely restricted. One meets only those whom one chooses to meet or cannot avoid. The rest are either blanked out of one's life or supplied at second hand by the media. When people from different sub-cultures are forced, by some accident, to spend more than a very short time in each other's company, the results can be extremely disturbing. The defences go up and communication is likely to remain on a very basic level. Normally and left to their own devices, people do their best to avoid such cross-cultural situations, but in such places as hospitals, doctors' and dentists' waiting-rooms and shops they may be forced into them. When this happens, language-labelling is likely to come into play very quickly. The choice and arrangement of words, and the manner in which they are spoken, divides the company into its social components as surely as the minutiae of dress and personal appearance. We are labelled from top to toe, and never more surely than when we speak.

It is not only what we say that matters. What we do not say is equally important, possible more so. The complex of the said and the unsaid, the concealed thought and the uttered thought, the accepted and the rejected is what splits one group off from another. One can, in fact, learn a great deal about the differences between one social group and another by confronting group A with a list of words and phrases commonly used by group B, and discovering why members of group A would not use group B expressions or, equally significantly, why they believe they would not use them. We shall investigate this very interesting phenomenon later in the present chapter.

In the case of English, which is a worldwide language, group A may well be in, say, San Francisco or Dallas and group B in Manchester or Sydney, and in such cases, where one group is being asked to comment on certain details or aspects of the language of another, much more than mere vocabulary is involved. Nearly all Americans are distinguished or handicapped, according to one's point of view, by a remarkably coarse ear, which is probably the result of a levelling process brought about by the mixture of races which has gone to make up the American nation. Out of this speech-cauldron came a form of language which concentrated on basic communication between members of a population which was socially and geographically extremely mobile. The subtleties of speech which had characterised the much more stable British society for generations had little place or point in America. They were undemocratic, as the Americans understood the term, and there was no time for them.

As Donald Davie pointed out in a brilliantly perceptive article on the subject, in America you have to make 'the context of your speech do everything that in Britain might be managed merely by the tone of it'.[26] The American voice and the American ear, he goes on to say, is remarkably insensitive – 'the ear's not hearing finely stops the voice from speaking finely, or vice-versa'.

This, as Davie points out, has important consequences, especially in the relation between the spoken and the written language. 'Sarcasm', he says, 'is managed by Americans through figurations of context, not intonation: in terms of the written, not the spoken language. They are, by no choice of their own, a very *literary* people; it's written English that they have to go to when they want to define their social place.' and the poor ear is a prime cause of another national disadvantage. 'This coarseness of the American ear explains why so many Americans are slow and incompetent at learning to speak foreign languages.'

Even more important, perhaps, is a fundamental difference between the English reader and the American reader. The undiscriminating, untuned ear from which Americans suffer –

explains their bewildered impatience with the aspect of literary English which we define, following I. A. Richards, as 'tone'. For 'tone' means ultimately 'tone of voice'. It describes a dimension of written English which requires, if we are to register the fluctuations of meaning within it, that the reader translate written English into spoken English by imagining a tone of

voice in which the written words would be said; and the voice
that says them has to be British, because only in British speech
can intonation do as much work, by way of defining social
situations and relationships, as the literary critic's understanding of 'tone' requires it to do.

This means, he goes on, 'that to a British reader most American
writing is either colloquial or stilted; a conversational style, which
ideally treads between the spoken and the written language,
drawing on both – this, which ever since Addison has been for the
British writer a sought-after norm of ease and plainness but also
of urbane insult, just isn't to be looked for in most American writing, though one or two New Yorkers in every generation seem to
manage it.'

There is perhaps a little exaggeration here – some Americans
must have a finer ear than others – but, in general, Donald
Davie's argument is well founded and reasonable. In the home
market, North America, the problem is as small or as great as
Americans choose to make it, but the situation is rather different
when parts of the American language are exported.

There are sections of, say, British society – sub-cultures –
which are so heavily Americanised in thinking and feeling that
they are able to absorb new American expressions easily, almost
instinctively. One could instance the pop-music and film worlds,
with their associated journalists, and some branches of business,
advertising and public relations. Here, a fondness for things
American goes with the job. But, although the people concerned
may think roughly as Americans think and may have worked in
America and with Americans, they have usually grown up in a
British atmosphere, surrounded by the British way of using words
and with British speech-tunes running through their heads. They
may have many superficial American characteristics – vocabulary, removing their jacket in the office or in the car, loosening
their tie to show how hard they are working, eating with a fork,
taking salad with everything, demanding iced water – but their
intonation, their 'tone', will, in the vast majority of cases, betray
their essential Britishness.

It is important to emphasise this, because it goes a long way
towards explaining why so many Americanisms continue to sound
foreign outside their country of origin, not unlike 'le weekend' in
French. They are linguistic shipwrecked sailors, floating peril-

ously on rafts in an ocean of non-American culture. Sometimes the ocean will allow them to drift towards the safety of the mainland, where many of them will settle and eventually become naturalised, but more often they will simply sink and drown.

There are, it is true, those people who pretend to be totally citizens of the world, with no national cultural allegiances and therefore nothing to mark them as citizens of this country or that. Their loyalties, they would say, are to this or that movement, belief or code of conduct, which acknowledges neither frontiers nor nationality. Their friends and allies, the people they understand and who understand them, are stretched out across the world, no matter whether the core of their common culture is homosexuality or the stock market, drugs or the anti-nuclear crusade, athletics or pop music. Among the English-speaking countries, each of these cultural bands will be defined and distinguished by a special stock of words and a special way of using them, a masonic language which outsiders can read and hear without comprehending.

No doubt there is a good deal of truth in this. Like will usually understand like better than unlike and certain shared characteristics of speech and appearance can get mutual comprehension and sympathy quickly on its way. But it is a delusion to believe that nationality is immaterial and that the social classes and subcultures which surround one's own can be disregarded. One is formed, shaped and motivated to a great extent by constantly reacting against people different from oneself. The people actually outside the cage make it easier for the monkey to be sure of his identity. Spectators gazing into another cage five thousand miles away cannot have the same effect.

Even in the age of the aeroplane and the multinational company, one cannot escape from the values and prejudices of one's own society. Superficially, the drug addict, the business executive, the tennis professional, the film producer, the pop fan, the academic may appear to be the same animal in America, Britain and Australia, interchangeable between one country and another, but in fact there are, for those with an interest in cultural minutiae, very significant differences between the national breeds. For all their travelling about and for all their common jargon and common appearance, they are, often in subtle ways, different, because the shape, size, influence, conflicting pressures and balance of the other sub-cultures in their own countries are different. Thyme put into one kind of soup does not produce quite the same effect as thyme in another.

The facts of cultural context cannot be overemphasised in any discussion of language. Whether we like it or not, we are all, young and old, educated and uneducated, identified by language labels, which involve the how and the where quite as much as the what. It is very difficult for a non-native to be fully sensitive to such labels and to their probable effect.

For an excellent example of this, take the highly successful *Private Eye* parodies of the style of Denis Thatcher, the amiable husband of the British Prime Minister. Clubman, Britain-for-the-British, all-foreigners-are-lunatics, Denis Thatcher is an agreeable survival of a breed of Englishman who epitomised the golf club and the officers' mess of the period between the wars, and the anonymous author of his 'Dear Bill' letters in *Private Eye* catches the idiom to perfection.

After the Royal Wedding in July 1981, Mrs Thatcher's husband was hoping to join his friend in 'a few celebratory tinctures', but instead had to attend an official function at which he had to 'pass around the peanuts for every coon and dervish in creation'. At the ceremony itself, he observed that the wife of the President of the United States was 'obviously pretty miffed at being put in Row H', and that a celebrated New Zealand opera singer of Maori blood – 'this dusky songstress from Down Under' – 'warbles on for bloody hours'. His friend, he was sure, would have been comfortably watching the proceedings on television, 'snort in hand'.

As he looks at the rest of the current political news and gossip, he notes that the Chancellor of the Exchequer 'is up for the one-way ticket to Siberia', that another Minister is 'a slimy little creep' and 'an oily little blighter', that Sir Charles Forte, 'the little chap with the moustache who runs the hotel chain', has said something rather foolish.

At the outfitters, where he had gone to hire morning dress for the occasion, he had been surrounded and kept waiting by 'a crowd of sambos, chinks and every other of the fifty-seven varieties hiring medals by the barrowload'. The Foreign Secretary had blundered to such an extent that the Spanish Royal Family had refused to attend the wedding, 'and he's now being pissed on from a great height by HRH'.[27]

One could always say, of course, that the 'Dear Bill' letters are caricature, and certainly they have been converted into highly successful theatre,[28] which suggests that the language may be somewhat more highly coloured than that of Mr Thatcher's ordinary daily speech. But, by moving in the right circles, one does meet people – always men – who do in fact talk like this. Expressions like 'miffed', 'coons', 'darkies', 'God rot his socks', 'toddle off to the sherbet cupboard', 'a stiff brownie and water', and 'chin chin, old fruit' come naturally to them and help to bind them together into a congenial body of like-minded people. 'A stiff brownie and water' is just as unmistakable a language label for them as 'dig' and 'vibes' have been for the rock/hippy sections of society. They are essentially words to be used between friends, cultural markers. But, for the full effect, one has to be able to imagine, hear mentally, the voice in which they are spoken. The accent, intonation, pausing are an essential part of the label, which is another way of saying that the printed dictionary provides a terribly inadequate record for posterity. The next big step forward in lexicography must surely be the dictionary with a keyed tape supplement.

CHAPTER THREE
Pop Music as a Cultural Carrier

'Music', Colin MacInnes decided in the late 1950s, '*is* our culture.'[1] It was a perceptive thing to say at the time, because the infrastructure of what MacInnes meant by 'music' – pop music – was still incomplete and fairly primitive. Transistor radios, the pop fan's essential personal weapon, were only just beginning to come on to the market, tape-recorders and record-players were still heavy and expensive, rock 'n' roll had only very recently crossed the Atlantic, discos were not yet born. The world was still, in fact, a fairly quiet place.

Since then, pop music and everything associated with it has become the main cultural diet of teenagers throughout the world and, as teenagers have grown up, of a steadily increasing number of nostalgic adults as well. It has become the focus of a complex youth sub-culture, determining values, ambitions, language and clothes. What pop musicians do, wear and say has become automatically desirable and right. Aiming at classlessness and universal appeal, they have proved to be one of the great divisive forces in society, super-heroes to the young and monsters of idiocy, depravity and corruption to a high proportion of their elders.

The older popular culture, described and to some extent idealised and romanticised by Richard Hoggart in *The Uses of Literacy*, met the needs of people who, one the whole, accepted society as it was. Their songs, like those of the Army during the First World War, were a way of making life tolerable. Since one could not reckon to change the essential shape and character of society, except perhaps very slowly and in small details, one might as well laugh at it and make the best of it. Pop culture, on the other hand, was, at least in its early stages, a form of protest. It made a strong appeal to people who saw few opportunities for themselves in the kind of world which had produced, reared and disappointed them. There has been no better description of it than that by George Melly, who was well qualified to understand what was happening. Born at just the right time, 1926, so that he was between two generations when the war ended, and in just the right place, Liverpool, he had been a sailor, an art gallery assistant and a singer before he became a writer and critic. He was not so much classless as poised between classes, the perfect cultural middleman.

'Pop culture', in Melly's analysis, 'is for the most part non-reflective, non-didactic, dedicated only to pleasure. It changes constantly, because it is sensitive to change, indeed it could be said that it is sensitive to nothing else. Its principal faculty is to catch the spirit of its time and translate this spirit into objects or music or fashion or behaviour. It could be said to offer a comic strip which compresses and caricatures the social and economic forces at work within our society. It draws no conclusions. It makes no comments. It proposes no solutions. It admits to neither past nor future, not even its own.'[2]

It was and still is essentially adolescent, both in its rejection of all tradition and all existing values, and in its awareness that it belongs to a stage in one's life which cannot last for ever. It represents the dream-world of the working class boy or girl destined for a lifetime of dull, meaningless work, a dream-world which can actually come true for those who become successful singers or musicians. As Melly shrewdly observes, there is such a thing, too, as adult pop, 'the swinging life as mirrored in the advertisements in the colour supplements', but this is largely middle- or upper-class fantasy, the fantasy of people with quite a lot of money, but never enough.

Pop culture has never been confined to music, but its art and its writing bear a strong resemblance to its music. All three draw their imagery instinctively from the more plebeian aspects of daily life – they belong, in David Sylvester's phrase, to a coke-culture, not a wine-culture – and they have all thrown the values and beliefs of the past overboard. Pop is essentially a lower-grade supermarket culture, and like the apples which are most esteemed at this level of retailing, it is carefully packaged, evenly graded and brightly coloured, but it has little real flavour. Crude and mindless as it has been so far, it is, even so, a genuine culture, in the sense that in grows spontaneously out of the dreams, hopes and feelings of real people. It is not imposed from above.

How classless pop culture has been is a matter of much argument. What is less debatable is that, so far as Britain is concerned, it began in the mid-1950s with the arrival of Tommy Steele on the scene, and that it coincided with a level of teenage prosperity that had never been seen before. Its predecessors, often referred to nowadays as pre-pop, were quite different. In the 1930s, with low wages and high unemployment, popular music was palais-de-danse music. It was the age of the big bands and of soft, warm, sentimental tunes to dance to and to croon, and the harder times were, the more escapist and make-believe the people's music was.[3] There was nothing that one could call teenage music then, nothing that puzzled adults and that teenagers could identify themselves with. They had to like, or dislike, the same songs, the same tunes, the same performers that their parents liked. The successful singers and bandleaders in those days were nearly always usually well on into their 30s before people began to hear about them.

The first significant exception to the rule was Frank Sinatra, who rose to prominence in the early 1940s, when he was still in his mid-20s, very old by present standards, but a miracle for the time. He was certainly a heart-throb, possibly the first heart-throb, but he was not exactly a teenage idol in the modern sense, and assuredly he was not a protester. He sang the same ballad-type songs as everyone else did and he appeared with the conventional and well-liked bands. But he had the advantage of picture-postcard good looks and he knew how to use his soulful eyes to great effect. Most of his fans were women in their 20s and 30s, with a few younger, and in wartime America, when no one, it is true, was quite normal, they screamed and fainted for him, which was something quite new in show business and a very long way indeed from the decorum and ritual of the palais de danse.

In looking at the way pop culture developed, one has to consider both the American seed and the variety of native soils outside America on to which that seed fell, sprouted and grew. That the origins, the seed, are to be found in the United States and among black musicians, is beyond doubt. What has become known as revivalist jazz, a product of the early and mid-1940s, can now be seen to have been a false start. Like pop, it was a spontaneous growth and, at least in its early years, had no commercial support. Also like pop, it was the centre of a life-style which made clear to the outside world that its practitioners and fans had an identity of their own: they were different. But, very different from pop, it looked backwards for its inspiration; it was trying to revive and reinterpret a golden age which lay in the past. Its enthusiasts were mostly well into their 20s, with more than a sprinkling of much older people and of those with good jobs and plenty of money. It was odd, and it was not a majority taste, but it was respectable. Most important of all, in view of later develop-ments, it contained little or no overtly sexual element. It was romantic.

Modern jazz, the creation of the late 1940s, was quite a different affair. It was contemporary through and through and made no concessions at all to nostalgia. It made its way under the title of bebop or bop, and it was brought into being by what one can think of as almost a school, although a small school, of black musicians in New York, who set out from the beginning to enlarge the harmonies and rhythms of jazz. They were aggressive-ly and unashamedly black, totally hostile to the idea of making money by playing to admiring whites. The Uncle Tom image was repulsive and impossible for them and they did everything they could to make plain their contempt for conventional attitudes in every field. Many of them, consciously if not deliberately, destroyed themselves with drugs. They were neither a happy nor a contented breed.

They could be only partly imitated abroad, for the good reason that they were black and the people who tried to follow their example were mostly white. But their white disciples did all the right things. They took to hard drugs, they wore dark glasses and they tried to walk and stand like their black American idols did, often becoming more than a little ridiculous in the process. There was no problem, either, in copying their manner of speaking but, however perfect the imitation, there could hardly help being something slightly absurd about white English musicians playing the part of American blacks. Modern jazz, none the less, did much to take the hard drug habit across the Atlantic. And modern jazz, plus the electric guitar, brought sex unequivocally into music.

The pioneers were on the scene by the late 1940s. There was T-Bone Walker, for instance, one of the first blues players to use the new-style technique of guitar and amplifier. 'As he played', said someone who watched him in action in Chicago, 'Walker would bop up and back across the wires, do the splits, and, man he could strut just like a burlesque queen. He would hold his guitar behind his neck, push it between his legs, and then, crouching low, begin to grind it against his groin. He made it clear that the electric guitar equalled sex.'[4] Curiously, the visual potential of the instrument with the most sexual of all shapes, the tenor saxophone, does not seem to have been realised until this time, despite the great musical popularity of the instrument in the 1920s and 1930s. Seen in retrospect, the period between the wars appears as one of extraordinary innocence.

Skiffle was another false start. In the early and mid-1950s it had a considerable following, both in Britain and the States, but, from a social point of view, its audience was not very wide. 'It had nothing to say to the Teddy boys. It in no way touched those who were looking for a music rooted in either sex or violence. It seemed, from the off, a bit folksy and tended to attract gentle creatures of vaguely left-wing affiliations. It appealed immediately to very young children, a quality which, in other pop movements, took a considerable time. Like revivalist jazz then, although being a vocal music it took less application to appreciate, it was in no way an anti-social movement. There were no skiffle riots.'[5]

Rock 'n' roll was fundamentally different. To begin with, the name was entirely sexual. It had been used by black blues-singers to detail love-making years before it became identified with a dance beat, and by 1948 it was being used in songs to describe both love-making and dancing. In 1951 a straight dance song, 'We're Gonna Rock', was something of a watershed, in that it had no obviously sexual implications, and in 1948 the American disc jockey, Alan Freed, who built an enormous reputation almost entirely on rock 'n' roll, called his regular radio show *Moondog's Rock and Roll Party*. But, as a musical genre, rock 'n' roll did not really hit the commercial music market until 1953, when Bill Haley and his Comets recorded 'Crazy Man Crazy'. This was the first rock 'n' roll song to reach the national charts in America and its popularity revealed that a new audience was forming itself. White youngsters had come over in droves to what had previously been very much black, even parochially black, music. Rock 'n' roll went into the juke boxes and the mass record market.

Haley was a curious phenomenon. In no sense could he be

called a teenage idol. His career up to that point had been as a country and western music singer and he was distinctly getting on in years. But, with the ground well manured by 'Crazy Man Crazy', he launched 'Rock Around the Clock' in the spring of 1954. After twelve months it was a hit in America and very soon afterwards in Britain. After that it went on to conquer the world. The record eventually sold 15 million copies and with it pop music had unmistakably arrived.

But the pop hero had not. Haley was obviously too old to play the role, but providence turned up in the shape of Elvis Presley, the Great Teenage Property, the universal hero, the rallying point for adolescent yearnings. He had everything that was required for successful promotion – youth, frenzied energy, sexual charisma, arrogance and, in public at least, a total disregard for convention and tradition. The fact that he was privately an exceedingly unpleasant person, who became steadily more disagreeable as he grew older and richer, was of no importance whatever. In front of the crowds, the cameras and the microphones he was unbeatable, and his fans built a mystique around him that the unbeliever found, and still finds, totally incomprehensible. No outsider, no interfering adult, could penetrate his mysteries. He was the central figure of a teenage freemasonry.

Once Presley was there as the great cult figure, teenagers became a movement, or perhaps one should say, a large proportion of them did. They developed their own international style in clothes, habits and language. The fact that Presley was American helped considerably, partly because he appeared to be classless and partly because he functioned as a white black, the perfect skin colouring for the teenage god.

The music that surrounded the god was, from a purely musical point of view, simple to the point of puerility. This was an advantage, rather than the reverse. All that mattered was the noise and aggressiveness. One not so much listened to it as felt it. The number of decibels generated by a rock 'n' roll performance was, to anyone coming into it from outside, crucifying, and later, in its recorded form at discos, even worse, because the space available was much less than in the concert hall. It has left a permanent mark, the scars of initiation rites, on the boys and girls who were proud to immerse themselves in it. They have gone partly deaf in their thousands, and their hearing will take rock 'n' roll to the grave, as a memento of the Great Teenage Rebellion, the determination of the young to go their own way. If they had all decided to cut off the lobes of their ears or poke a stick through their nostrils, the marking could hardly have been more definite.

The actual words sung, screamed, chattered and bawled by Elvis Presley and the lesser idols were only fractionally more basic than the music. To say that they were banal would be to give them a dignity and a status to which they are not entitled. At their best they were repetitious clichés, and at their worst – and the worst was the norm – they were gibberish. But this, given the context, was a positive merit. It was deliberate, a code understood only by teenagers, and the words and the music together formed a protective barrier against the adult world.

To assume that the 'lyrics' which came from the mouths of rock 'n' roll singers had meaning in themselves as words is to miss the point altogether. As I have said earlier, they were not intended to be impressive on the page, or even to make sense. They existed only to make it possible for the voice to operate, and they were not necessarily the most important of the devices a skilled performer had at his command. He could, for example, sigh, change tone and volume, laugh, grunt and produce a rich variety of noises which presumably were intended to indicate the emotions welling up within him and which demanded some form of urgent public outlet.

It may well be that in the past noises have not had the understanding and the cultural prestige they deserve. What pop music has done, however, is to downgrade the importance of using connected words with skill and sensitivity. If grunts and moans and other farmyard modes of communication can do everything that is required, why bother about a careful choice of words and fine shades of meaning? To use words well and to have an abundance of words at one's disposal could indeed be the badge to the enemy. All that one needs is a supply of code words. The initiates, those who belong, know the code and how to use it. Those outside the group are almost certain to get it wrong. They are always falling into the trap of using yesterday's in-words without realising that these words have already been replaced and that the real people are laughing at the imposters for their ignorance.

Rock 'n' roll did not have to stand on its own, as a cultural freak. It found a powerful ally in the American cinema industry, which saw a market for films which focused attention on the conflict between the generations. Two films stood out in this respect, *The Wild One,* which appeared in 1954, with Marlon Brando as its centrepiece, and *Rebel without a Cause* (1955), which was built round James Dean. Both films had poor, crude plots, but the feelings of frustration and violence which Brando and Dean were able to put across provided something a teenage audience could understand and sympathise with. Everything about these two actors – their dress, way of walking, facial expressions, speech and general attitude to life and the world – was a model to which many boys at least – the attitude of girls is less easy to categorise – were strongly attracted.

Marlon Brando, James Dean, Johnnie Ray, Bill Haley – the people whom Jeff Nuttall once called 'the brute heroes, the hipster-heroes, the pain-heroes' – made a special appeal to a particular section of the teenage group, the motorcyle cowboys, the wild ones, who made a cult of violence. When Haley and his band appeared in England and at the first showing of Elvis Presley films, the audiences celebrated by cutting the seats to pieces with razors. This was not intended as a protest against the performance or against the management of the theatre. It was simply a way of expressing gratitude to Haley or Presley or whoever it might be for making their violence available to the audience, a ritualistic gesture.

It is worth mentioning, perhaps, that in the way it reacted to the current teenage mood the American film industry was much less conservative and timid than either the music industry or the broodcasting industry. After thirty years of interracial struggles in both Britain and the United States, it is not easy today to remember how very white-dominated music and radio were in the 1940s and early 1950s, in their values, personalities and atmosphere. In the 1950s, American film companies were prepared to allow white actors to use black speech-styles long before radio showed the same degree of tolerance. In the 1940s, words like 'flip', 'cat', 'jive', 'square' and the other bebop expressions were still black talk. Rock 'n' roll and the films linked to it turned them into white talk. Such a change is comparable to the revolution in attitudes which allowed nudity and four-letter words into the London West End theatre.

With pop culture now so thoroughly internationalised, and the American victory now so complete as to be no longer noticeable, it takes a considerable effort of the imagination to realise just how appealing American culture was to young people in Britain in the 1940s and early 1950s. America's comics and books and its Western and gangster films made no serious demands on the brain. The relationships between their characters was simple and direct, without the familiar British complications of accent, class and status, experiences and feelings were open and easy to grasp, ambition was boundless and unshackled, and success and money went to the strong and single-minded. With rock 'n' roll to add a musical dimension to the desirability of the American way of life, Britain, so far as the younger members of the working class were concerned appeared well on the road to becoming another State of the Union.

The promoters of pop soon found themselves faced with a tactical problem of some size. The root of the difficulty was the fact that the human race consists of two sexes and that any entrepreneur in the entertainment world throws away half his potential market if he pleases one sex and antagonises and bores the other. Traditionally and for good reasons girls, especially ordinary working girls, expected their films, their reading and their music to contain a strong romantic element. They wanted, perfectly understandably, to be given a temporary escape from the routine and drabness of their day-to-day lives.

But rock 'n' roll was completely and totally unsubtle and unromantic, a male-dominated thing from beginning to end. Haley and Presley were crude sensualists; according to their philosophy, women were mere chattels and men had the right to uncontrolled promiscuity. They quite deliberately incited working-class boys to blind, mindless violence and vandalism. This from the promoter's point of view, was a dangerous situation. If he were to make money out of pop, he had to find some means of bringing order and at least the appearance of fairness and civilisation into the situation, while at the same time preserving the illusion of a never-ending revolt against the customs and attitudes of the adult world. It was not an easy task.

The problem was eventually solved in a most interesting, ingenious and unscrupulous way. George Melly, who experienced the results at first hand, analyses the technique in this way:

> The trick is to shift the emphasis so that the pop idol, originally representing a masculine rebel, is transformed into a mas-

turbation fantasy object for adolescent girls. The shrieking, squirming audience in the process of self-induced mass-orgasm is, depending on one's viewpoint, unattractive or disturbing or sad, but it is controllable. The individual girl mooning over her pop-hero is, for most parents, irritating enough to convince her that she is in revolt, but it is in most cases both temporary and unimportant. Furthermore, this mass-shrieking and solitary mooning are, from the authorities' viewpoint, preferable to the growth of male aggression on whatever level and, on the promotional side, has the commercial advantage of gradually extending its range to include a younger and wider audience before losing its momentum.[6]

There are those who believe, with some justice, that pop is not what it was, that what started as revolt degenerated into mere style, with each successive wave of pop music appealing to an even younger age-group. But it is misleading to regard British and American teenagers as interchangeable, whether the date is 1950, 1970 or 1980. In the 1950s, the British teenager, as distinct from the British adolescent, was typically working or lower middle class. In America, in the same decade, he came from further up the social scale, a development which took another ten years to establish itself in Britain. Until the Beatles arrived on the scene in the 1960s, the source and inspiration of pop music and of everything that went with it was firmly American. The Beatles reversed the flow and 'established a dialogue between the two cultures which is still open'.[7]

It took the Beatles a remarkably brief two years, from 1962 to 1964, to reach the top, and it is worth remembering that they received their MBEs for 'services to export'. The award and the citation showed a degree of imagination and wit sadly rare among Government officials. The Beatles' exports were, of course, partly cultural and partly a matter of sordid commerce. The sales of their records brought a great deal of money back to Britain and some of it, of course, found its way to the Beatles themselves.

The real historical significance of the Beatles is difficult to discuss rationally, let alone determine, while the cult that grew up around them is still so much alive. One of the most balanced and intelligent assessments so far of their place in the postwar cultural scene is to be found in *The Times*'s long obituary[8] of John Lennon, after his assassination in New York at the end of 1980.

The Beatles, said *The Times*, 'created paroxyms of enthusiasm which rivalled and surpassed anything that had gone before them in the short history of rock and roll. Hairstyles, styles of dress, even styles of speaking – for the first time a transatlantic twang ceased to be a *sine qua non* for pop performers – followed in their wake.' They were a great sucess in America and 'completely wrested the palm from the country where rock and roll had been born and bred and which in those days seemed to have a prescriptive right to adjudicate on what was feasible and what was not in pop music. After the Beatles it was never again possible for British groups to think of themselves as the poor relations in pop music.'

The Beatles, the author of *The Times*'s obituary believed, rescued pop from the orgy of sheer noise into which it had sunk after the initial drive of Haley and Presley had exhausted itself. 'The Beatles brought a new musicality to pop music which succeeded in giving it a much wider appeal than it had had previously. In their genial, at any rate seldom less than pleasing, melodies and enticing, attractive harmonies, they somehow gave an impression of being more musically literate than any of their predecessors – although in fact none of the four could either read or write music.' This, together with their washed and tidy appearance, 'gave pop music a sudden entrée into quarters where it had previously been virtually a proscribed subject.'

Lennon himself was something of an intellectual. By comparison with the Haleys and the Presleys, who were crudely animal, he was a Great Brain. The period he spent at the Liverpool College of Art was significant, partly because it was an art college and partly because it was in the North of England.

The remarkable influx of Northern musical groups and singers into the pop field during the 1950s and 1960s – it is paralleled in the theatre, with actors like Albert Finney and Tom Courtenay – has done a great deal to break down British class and regional barriers. It became normal not to belong to London and the South-East. One did not have, like Gracie Fields and George Formby in previous generations, to caricature Northern life in order to be successful. Once a Northern accent had become incidental and no longer a mere peg for comedy, it could be regarded as more or less classless by people who did not speak it themselves, classless in the sense that one found it difficult to place those who used it in any particular social or educational group. But it was unlikely to be taken over by people who did not belong to Liverpool or Bradford or wherever the accent might be located. The disc jockey, John Peel, was a notable exception. Peel was very much a public-school product. Like his *Private Eye* and *That Was The Week That Was* contemporaries, Richard Ingrams, William Rushton and Paul Foot, he had been at Shrewsbury. He chose to speak in a very flat Liverpudlian, which was acceptable from him, but not from his many lesser imitators. He was in demand for TV commercials, including those for Marmite and fish fingers.

The influence of Cliff Richard, a year or two before the appearance of the Beatles, was rather different. In due course, his religious beliefs and his much-commented-on wholesome appearance became important, but in the early days it was his speaking voice that really mattered. Before him, all British pop singers sounded what they were, solidly working-class. Cliff Richard introduced something new, a bland, completely classless way of talking. It caught on and it was widely imitated. David Frost was quick to pick it up. 'It has become', reported Nik Cohn, at the end of the 1960s, 'the dominant success voice.'[9]

The social influence of the art schools was nationwide. They had been greatly expanded during the 1950s and they provided a very congenial atmosphere for boys and girls with fairly vague intellectual interests and a conviction that the more formal and demanding courses at a university were not for them. Even before the war they had a tradition of a certain Bohemian classlessness, and this, mixed with a general sympathy with pop music and pop art and design, made them natural centres of political and artistic ferment during what one might call the Beatle period. They were responsible for creating many of the most original teenage dress fashions and what was almost conventional style inside the art schools was often considered revolutionary outside. The Beatles' original shaggy-dog, brushed-forward hairstyles were art school. They attracted a great deal of publicity when the Beatles began to be well known, but in the art schools they had been commonplace for a long time and, within this milieu, hardly worth commenting on. The art schools produced a high proportion of the members of Britain's leading pop groups in the 1960s. The Beatles, the Animals, the Rolling Stones, the Kinks, the Who and the Yardbirds all included former art students.

From the point of view of authority and the Establishment, the art students did not become really troublesome until long after the reputation of the Beatles had become firmly established. The Hornsey School of Art was a particular hot spot in the late 1960s. The rebellious students were eventually locked out of the college, and after they had protested vigorously about this outside Haringey Town Hall, a local councillor, Alderman Bains, achieved temporary fame in a much-publicised interview. 'This', he told the world, 'is a pure Chinese Red Guard effort and we are not having it. A bunch of crackpots, here in Haringey, or in Grosvenor Square, or Paris, or Berlin, or Mexico, can never overthrow an established system. We, the ordinary people, the nine-to-five, Monday-to-Friday, semi-detached suburban wage-earners, we *are* the system. We are not victims of it. We are not slaves to it. We are it, and we like it. Does any bunch of twopenny-halfpenny kids think they can turn us upside down? They'll learn.'[10]

It was no accident that British art students should have been central figures in youth protest movements. In values, attitudes and habits, the art colleges had changed faster and more thoroughly than society as a whole, and their students consequently saw themselves, not as observers of the new culture, but as people who had helped to produce it.

It is easy to overlook the fact that neither pop culture nor its personalities are static. The culture itself is constantly changing and even world institutions like the Beatles progressed. As early as 1968, when the Beatles were at the height of their fame and riches, it was apparent to one unusually perceptive observer that they were no longer conventional chart material at all. Adrian Mitchell said in a broadcast:

They've already shown some courage in a traditionally cowardly trade for in pop music the aim is to be loved by everyone, villains included. Maybe it was foolhardiness when they filmed their own Magical Mystery Tour. It contained some images – policemen holding hands on top of a concrete bunker or shelter, while the Beatles played below in Disney masks – which were way beyond the heads of most of the critics. The progress of their songs from 'Please Please Me' (instantly likeable, and who, at that time, could ask for anything more?) to 'Penny Lane' (poetry) and 'A Day in the Life' and 'I am the Walnut' (adventurous poetry) has been an exciting voyage to follow.

After all, everyone knew Francis Chichester wasn't going to fall off the edge of the world, but the Beatles might.[11]

Perhaps one can say, with hindsight, that the Beatles' greatest contribution was to explode the myth that the working classes were intrinsically more interesting, real and honest than the middle classes, the myth which had been fostered, if not created, by *Look Back in Anger*, *Saturday Night and Sunday Morning*, *The Loneliness of the Long-Distance Runner* and other books and films of the genre. The Beatles had no ideology; they were pushing no social message, making no outspoken criticisms of the established order of society. They implied, rather than stated, a criticism of convention and they showed no dissatisfaction at all with wealth and fame. They presented working-class boys and girls as free and happy with their lot, fond of making themselves as comfortable as possible and enjoying every opportunity to demolish shams and pomposity. They found politics and political protests boring and kept well clear of anything that smacked of a 'movement'. They poked fun at themselves publicly, they admired luxury and were not at all reticent about their pleasure at being rich. Their male and their female fans were equally numerous and they themselves were as interesting and agreeable to listen to as to look at, both very rare qualities in the pop-music world.

Perhaps one could sum it up by saying that the Beatles became rich and secure enough to be able to laugh at it all. They were the aristocrats of pop and they could afford to have the aristocrat's age-old privilege of mocking the source of his wealth.

Pop culture, for all its dislike of the printed word, depended a great deal on magazines for its growth and cohesion. Publications like *Rolling Stone*, *Melody Maker* and *New Musical Express* were the pop world's channels of communication. They sold in large quantities, but the people who read them were by no means indentical with the fans who went crazy at concerts. They were, for one thing, rather older and they had more money. By 1971 the American *Rolling Stone* was selling 250,000 copies an issue in the United States and Canada, and 25,000 in Britain. In the same year the two main British-based publications, *Melody Maker* and *New Musical Express*, had circulations of 171,000 and 147,000 respectively, which was good business for a magazine.

Their editors had a pretty accurate idea of who their readers were. In 1969, the editor of *Rolling Stone*, Jann Wenner, put it this way:

> The average *Rolling Stone* reader is twenty-two years old. Seventy per cent of them are male. About fifty per cent are in college. They are quite wealthy. We reckon that they account for about half the record sales in America. They buy between four and five albums a month. I think the whole thing about the new youth being anti-materialistic is bullshit. Our readership spends quite a bit of money on high fidelity equipment. Twenty-two per cent of them own Volkswagens.[12]

The editor of the *Melody Maker* would probably not have been able to give quite the same picture of his readership but, allowing for the differences between Britain and America, the overall pattern would not have differed a great deal. It amounts to saying that the people who buy such papers regularly constitute a pop intelligentsia. Their part in the movement is to read and theorise about it and to listen to records in their own homes, leaving most of the up-front activity to the teenage coolies. Pop itself, like the Soviet Union, may pride itself on presenting a classless image to the world, but there are certainly classes and hierarchies within it. It is not all of a piece.

The kind of advertising carried by these papers provides solid clues to the readership. It is clearly aimed today, as it was ten years ago, at people with money, not at an impoverished proletariat, and each issue contains an enormous amount of it, which helps to keep the price low.[13] Most of the articles continue to be about pop music, but the field has widened a good deal in recent years. An issue of *New Musical Express* in 1981, for instance, contained a by no means hostile article about Prince Charles and the then Lady Diana Spencer, and another on 'Return of the Anti-Nazi League'. What the publishers seem to be cautiously developing is a magazine of general interest for readers with a strong interest in pop music and with vaguely 'progressive', anti-racist attitudes. It seems a sensible policy to follow. The market is clearly there.

Through its publications, its practitioners and its followers, pop music has helped to bring about widespread changes in English speech during the past forty years. One could illustrate this by outlining the career of the word 'camp', which forms part of the vocabulary of very few people over 50, but which is widely used lower down the age-range. It symbolises the gulf between the generations.

'Camp' was originally a homosexual term. It meant 'obviously and often outrageously queer'. It was also applied approvingly to certain kinds of non-homosexual who appealed to homosexuals, and it was frequently, perhaps normally, used with what one might describe as a wink in the voice.

Christopher Isherwood, himself a homosexual, invented the term 'high-camp' and differentiated it from 'low-camp'. 'Low-camp' was 'a female impersonator imitating Marlene Dietrich in a seedy night-culb'; 'high-camp' carried no sexual overtones and meant 'possessing a confident theatricality'.

'Camp' was then taken over by pop, which kept its slightly mocking overtone, but redefined it to mean 'ridiculous, because dated' but, for this very reason, safe to approve of. Once something was 'camp', it presented no danger. It was tucked away inside inverted commas and one was not identified with it. And, through pop, not through homesexuals or Graham Greene, it became a word for the young and irreverent everywhere, until eventually it wore itself out through sheer boredom.

One could hardly end this chapter without mentioning punk, which in a way returns pop to its origins. It is the arch-protest, undertaken by people who were frightened that the original teenage revolution might have failed, or at least become so watered down that it no longer counted for anything. During the late 1970s and early 1980s, the punks, a largely British creation, have gone to great pains to ensure that society as a whole vehemently disapproves of them. They have cultivated an outrageous appearance, they have defended illiteracy and idleness, they have pushed profanity and obscenity to extremes. Yet, however much they may have satisfied their own yearning for rebellion and their eagerness to overthrow convention, it is doubtful if their message, if it is indeed a message, has reached the public at large, which continues to find them rather sinister figures of fun, rather than apostles of a revolution.

It is ironical that those who do not understand punk laugh at it, whereas those who write about it sympathetically are virtually unintelligible to those who are not already initiates and connoisseurs. Here, for example, is Dick Hebdige, doing his best to explain the pedigree of punk:

A new style was being created; combining elements from a whole range of heterogeneous youth styles. In fact, punk claimed a dubious pedigree. Strands from David Bowie and glitter-rock were woven together with elements from American proto-punk (the Ramones, the Heartbreakers, Iggy Pop, Richard Hill), from that faction within London pub-rock (the 101-ers, the Gorillas, etc.), inspired by the mod subculture of the 60s, from the Canvey Island 40s revival and the Southend r and b bands (Dr. Feelgood, Lewis, etc), from northern soul and rock reggae.[14]

Such an explanation is no doubt accurate and well-informed, but anyone without first-hand knowledge of the Ramones, Iggy Pop and the rest is likely to find it lacking in illumination, possibly a trifle inbred. There is a great deal that is masonic about the pop world, and deliberately so. Those who are within it understand and for them no explanations are necessary, and for outsiders any attempt to explain is pointless, because understanding is impossible. Pop is essentially for believers.

CHAPTER FOUR
The Lexicographer's Waterloo

In the late 1950s, J. Isaacs, who was a Professor of English at the University of London, attempted to discover an answer to a question which looks simple but which is, in fact, extremely difficult. 'What', he wanted to know, 'is a dictionary?' and he came to the conclusion that a definition was practically impossible, that a dictionary, which existed to provide definitions, was incapable of defining itself. He wrote:

> It all depends whether you are a dictionary-maker or a dictionary-user. The dictionary-user has certain needs. The dictionary-maker works on principles. But, as Dr. Johnson said 200 years ago, ordinary readers do not worry about principles, and 'know not any other use of a dictionary than that of adjusting orthography, or explaining terms of science or words of frequent occurrence or remote derivation'. You may use a dictionary to settle a bet, to see what a word means, how it is pronounced, how it is used, who invented it, when it was first used, whether it is still current or obsolete, whether it is standard English or dialect, or a technical term, or colloquial or slang, whether it is a nice word or a naughty word. It took a long time before all these things could be answered accurately in a single dictionary, more than 200 years, in fact.[1]

Professor Isaacs was flattering the modern dictionary-makers. 'All these things' have never yet been 'answered accurately in a single dictionary' and never will be. A word is not just 'used'; it is used by a wide range of people on a great variety of occasions. It may have a basic meaning, a central core of reference – a horse is clearly not a cow – but the personal and social overtones which form an essential part of a word in use are beyond the powers of a dictionary to record or convey. Always there is, or should be, the question 'to whom?' Pronounced by whom? Used by whom? Current for whom? Nice for whom? Naughty for whom?

Johnson, as Isaacs acknowledges, was completely honest in the matter. His principle was clear and he never deviated from it. He was 'using a dictionary to fix the standard of polite and elegant usage in language'.[2] Such a dictionary made sense. One could quarrel with the principle behind it, but one understood the kind of work one was consulting. With a modern dictionary one is always in doubt, mainly because its editor has two irreconcilable aims. Whatever he may claim, he is trying, at one and the same time, to recommend or at least indicate something he feels to be a desirable standard and to record usages which depart from the standard. He may believe that he is analysing and reporting on something he calls 'English', whereas what he is in fact doing is presenting his readers with English as it has appeared in print, and that is a very different commodity. The essential feature of Johnson, as of most other dictionaries, is that they are based on what can be discovered in books and, more recently, in news-papers and magazines. They ignore the all-important fact that language, for most people, is primarily speech. Print comes a very poor second. It is true that print often purports to reproduce speech, but in practice it transforms it to a greater or lesser extent in the process of getting it on to paper.

For this and other reasons – the need to have very short definitions, the age and personal prejudices of editors, the inability to know what kind of people will use the dictionary – even the best dictionary is an imperfect tool, imperfect, in many instances, to the point of being actually misleading. There are some words it cannot handle, except in a very rough and ready way, and there are others it prefers not to handle. There are expressions, contexts and connotations of which it is unaware. More seriously, every dictionary so far published introduces value-judgements; either explicitly or by their omission, some words and phrases are categorised as worse than others, which is as foolish and arrogant as saying that some sorts of weather are inferior or less desirable.

The sifting of the vocabulary of the mother-tongue in this way is both arbitrary and authoritarian. If a word or a meaning exists, or has existed at some time, one has a duty to record it, assuming that one's dictionary is intended to be comprehensive. To produce a specialised dictionary is, of course, a perfectly reasonable thing to do. A dictionary of engineering or botanical terms is entitled to be precisely that, a thin vertical slice through the language but, even then, its compiler may well decide to exclude what he considers 'colloquial' or 'popular' words, and to concentrate entirely on the up-market and purely technical vocabulary. Iris foetidissima might therefore be in, and Stinking Iris out, Chenopodium album in and Fat Hen out. One could always cheat, of course, by saying that a flower name and a botanical name are two quite different things but, whatever one's tactics and justification, to leave out Stinking Iris and Fat Hen would be a value-judgement. They would have been considered unworthy of a place in the dictionary, and if and when that happens the vertical slice becomes half a slice.

A general dictionary, however, does not purport to be a vertical slice through English or German or whatever the language may be. Its cut is essentially horizontal. Its words cover all subjects, all branches of human activity, but, whatever claims may be made for the new work – more entries, more up-to-dateness, more specialist advisers, more etymologies – the user of the dictionary is not in actual fact going to get the whole slice or anything like it. Whether deliberately or unconsciously, a selection process will have taken place between the raw language and the reader. The editor and his staff will have exercised their discretion and concealed their ignorance. Even when a word or meaning is on the files and passes the test for inclusion, it is very likely to be graded as 'obsolete', 'slang', 'taboo' or whatever other system of labels the particular dictionary may be using.

In making such a selection or in attaching such value-tickets, many subjective forces are at work, forces of which the reader is most unlikely to be aware. How old is the person responsible for each decision? Is it a he or a she? How wide an experience of people and human behaviour has he or she had? How tolerant, prudish, censorious, peculiar is he or she?

To allow or encourage an editor to use terms like 'colloquial' or 'taboo' is to put a dangerous tool into his hands. What, after all, do such words really mean? To whom are they intended to be helpful? What assumptions do they make?

The answer to all these fundamental questions is that, however much he might deny it, the editor expects his readers to be roughly like himself, with much the same standards of right and wrong, high and low, permitted and forbidden, socially acceptable and socially disreputable. If he and his friends would never use this or that word in the presence of ladies or in a railway compartment, 'taboo' is clearly called for, to protect the innocent from possible ostracism and misfortune. The fact that other kinds of people, especially the young and the less well educated, might react quite differently to the same words is not reckoned with.

This strange and fundamentally unscientific way of going about the business of dictionary-making is well illustrated by the use, and indeed existence, of the word 'slang'. The more I think about this word, the more nonsensical and unhelpful it seems. It does not relate to the world of English-speakers at all. It implies an authoritarian situation, in which one cultural group attempts to regulate the speech of the rest of the population, an Academy State in which some words and phrases are officially acceptable, others are less acceptable and others again are not acceptable at all. A dictionary planned and organised in this way is prescriptive, not descriptive, and that is against the spirit of our time, however welcome it may have been in Georgian or Victorian days.

The Oxford English Dictionary, in its revised, 1933, version, offers three principal definitions of slang. They are:

1. The special vocabulary used by any set of persons of a low or disreputable character; language of a low and vulgar type.
2. The special vocabulary or phraseology of a particular calling or profession; the cant or jargon of a certain class or period.
3. Language of a highly colloquial type, considered as below the level of standard educated speech and consisting either of new words or of current words employed in some special sense.

Ironically, the *Dictionary* quotes, under (2), a remark made by George Eliot, in *Middlemarch*. 'Correct English', she wrote – the date was 1870 – 'is the slang of prigs who write history and essays. And the strongest slang is the slang of poets.' The point has never been made better. 'Poets' is not, of course, to be interpreted in the narrow sense of 'people who write or compose poetry'. It means something much wider here, those who take pleasure in playing about with words and in squeezing new possibilities out of them, the irreverent users of language, who see it as the raw material of self-expression and communication, not as a strait-jacket of good manners, the experimenters. Such people, George

Eliot's 'poets', are the ones who keep a language alive. They need not be educated, in the formal sense, and they may well lead strange or far from respectable lives. They are certainly extremely unlikely to care in the least if the words they use easily and naturally are stigmatised as 'taboo', 'low', 'colloquial' or 'slang'.

The Oxford English Dictionary (*OED*) was a magnificent product of an extremely class-conscious society, conceived in Victorian times – the first editor began work in 1878 – and completed fifty years later. The last page went to the printer in 1928, which meant that by the time the *Dictionary* was complete the early part of it was half-a-century out-of-date, and the whole work was urgently in need of an overhaul. But the revision, when it came, was a revision of detail, not of philosophy or approach. The basic principles remained unchanged and, since they have influenced all subsequent dictionary-makers, it is worth looking at them with some care.

The editors first considered how their predecessors had set about the task of compiling a dictionary. They observed that the sixteenth and seventeenth century lexicographers had concentrated on the 'hard words' – that is, words built from foreign, usually Greek or Latin, components – and that one compiler borrowed generously from another, even to the extent of taking complete definitions from someone else's work.[3] The *OED* editors gave Dr Samuel Johnson full credit for the revolutionary principles on which his 1755 *Dictionary* had been based, and especially on his system of quoting authorities for each usage. What they did not acknowledge – perhaps it seemed too obvious to them – was their indebtedness to Johnson's aims.

Johnson was a classicist. He believed in the study, refinement and perfection of what already existed; change, for someone trained in this tradition, was a bad thing, to be resisted as far as possible. So, what he was attempting was, in his own words, 'a dictionary by which the pronunciation of our language may be fixed and its attainment facilitated; by which its purity may be preserved, its use ascertained, and its duration lengthened.'[4]

Johnson's explicit aim was to set standards and, above all, to decide which words were fit to form part of the English language and which were not. And once the standard of correctness was set and agreed on, there was little more to do, except to pounce unremittingly on those who wilfully or ignorantly broke the rules. These rules, he insisted, were not intended to be interpreted, stretched or discussed; they were to be observed. 'The one great end of this undertaking', he wrote of his *Dictionary*, 'is to fix the English language', to get it safely into harbour, after so many years of sailing about on the high seas without a compass.

By the time Johnson had settled down to his labours, fixing the mother-tongue had been a popular pursuit for some years. In 1698, Defoe praised the French Academy for its efforts to regulate the French language and proposed something similar in his own country, 'to encourage polite learning, to polish and refine the English tongue, to establish purity and propriety of style, and to purge it from all the irregular additions that ignorance and affectation have introduced and all those innovations in speech, if I may call them such, which some dogmatic writers have the confidence to foster upon their native language, as if their authority were sufficient to make their own fancy legitimate.'[5]

Not long afterwards, Jonathan Swift, in his *Proposal for Correcting, Improving and Ascertaining the English Tongue*, was writing in much the same vein. He regretted the 'corruptions' which had crept into the language and believed it was essential to have recognised authorities who would 'reform' our language and 'ascertain and fix it for ever'.[6]

A contemporary of Johnson's, Benjamin Martin, whose own very interesting and important dictionary[7] has been unreasonably overshadowed by Johnson's, was far more realistic. 'The pretence of fixing a standard to the purity and perfection of any language', he said, 'is utterly vain and impertinent, because no language as depending on arbitrary use and custom, can ever be permanently the same, but will always be in a mutable and fluctuating state; and what is deemed polite and elegant in one age, may be accounted uncouth and barbarous in another.'

And, by the time his *Dictionary* was published, even Johnson himself had come to feel that, in promising to 'fix our language', he had 'indulged expectation which neither reason nor experience can justify'. One should try to keep change at bay, but it was wise not to be optimistic of success. 'When we see men grow old and die at a certain time one after another, from century to century, we laugh at the elixir that promises to prolong life to a thousand years; and with equal justice may the lexicographer be derided, who, being able to produce no example of a nation that has preserved their words and phrases from mutability, shall imagine that his dictionary can embalm his language, and secure it from corruption and decay, that it is in his power to change sublunary nature, and clear the world at once from folly, vanity and affectation.'[8]

The editors of *The Oxford English Dictionary* certainly never believed that English could be, to use Johnson's term, 'embalmed':

> The living vocabulary is no more permanent in its constitution than definite in its extent. It is not today what it was a century ago, still less what it will be a century hence. Its constituent elements are in a state of slow but incessant dissolution and renovation. 'Old words' are ever becoming obsolete and dying out; 'new words' are constantly pressing in. And the death of a word is not an event of which the date can be readily determined. It is a vanishing process, extending over a lengthened period, of which contemporaries never see the end. Our own words never become obsolete; it is always the words of our grandfathers that have died with them. Even after we cease to use a word, the memory of it survives and the word itself survives as a possibility; it is only when no one is left to whom its use is still possible that the word is wholly dead. Hence, there are many words of which it is doubtful whether they are still to be considered as part of the living language; they are alive to some speakers, and dead to others. And, on the other hand, there are many claimants to admission into the recognised vocabulary (where some of them will certainly one day be received) that are already current coin with some speakers and writers, and not yet 'good English', or even not English at all, to others.[9]

It is a marvellous piece of prose, and good sense from beginning to end, yet it avoids the fundamental question, raised a century earlier by Johnson, 'Who judges the judges?' Consider the implications of the statement, 'there are many claimants to admission into the recognised vocabulary'. First, one has to ask, 'recognised' by whom? Given the period, the answer can only be 'by an unspecified, but perfectly well understood, body of educated, well-bred people who constitute the intellectual establishment, the Académie Britannique without a name'. One then has a picture of a situation not unlike that at the gates of Heaven, with a never-ending queue of candidates for admission, hoping with suspended breath and a racing pulse that their credentials will be recognised and that they will be given an entry visa. Such a concept was perfectly normal in the structured society which Britain was at that time and is no longer, a society in which people knew their place and had an automatic respect for those with a social position superior to their own, a society in which phrases like 'low', 'vulgar' and 'standard educated speech' had real meaning.

Most important from the point of view of the editors and publishers of *The Oxford English Dictionary*, they were able to assume, at least for the major thirteen-volume work, a public with taste, knowledge and background not dissimilar to their own. It was a reasonably homogeneous public, the members of which were exceptionally interested in language, almost certainly with a classical education and accustomed to taking care over their own speaking and writing. If the *OED* said a word was 'low', the meaning registered immediately. It was an expression they themselves would never use, something said by 'them', the uneducated, the bottom of the social pile, but never by 'us'.

With the gradual appearance of compressed versions of *The Oxford Dictionary*, this community of understanding and taste between provider and receiver became less certain. *The Shorter Oxford* must have had a wider range of users than its parents, *The Concise* wider still and *The Pocket* even wider. But, since the tone had already been set by the main work, this probably did not matter very much. As *The Oxford Dictionary* became progressively smaller and cheaper, the rarer words, the examples, and the history were squeezed out, but the process was essentially one of exclusion, not of addition. The specialised and exotic 'claimants to admission' found it harder to secure entry to *The Shorter*, *The Concise* and *The Pocket*, simply because there was less room for them, not because they were morally unfit to be in a good dictionary.

The men responsible for compiling *The Oxford English Dictionary* realised, like every other honest member of their profession, that every dictionary must be, to a greater or lesser extent, a compromise. It has to be marketable and it has to produce an adequate return on investment. If it is too big and therefore too expensive, it will not sell, and the size therefore has to be kept within commercially possible limits. This usually means that the editor is compelled to make sacrifices. Something has to go, if the work is to be published at all.

The successive editors of *The Oxford Dictionary*, Dr James Murray, Henry Bradley, W. A. Craigie and C. T. Onions, understood this perfectly well. A line had to be drawn somewhere, and the editors explained with complete honesty and clarity how they had set about solving the problem:

> The English Vocabulary contains a nucleus or central mass of many thousand words, whose 'Anglicity' is unquestioned; some of them only literary, some of them only colloquial, the great majority at once literary and colloquial – they are the *Common Words* of the language. But they are linked on every side with other words which are less and less entitled to this appellation, and which pertain ever more and more distinctly to the domain of local dialect, of the slang and cant of sets [10] and classes, of the peculiar technicalities of trades and processes, of the scientific terminology common to all civilised nations, of the actual languages of other lands and peoples.
>
> And there is absolutely no defining line in any direction: the circle of the English has a well-defined centre but no discernable circumference. Yet practical utility has some bounds, and a Dictionary has definite limits: the lexicographer must, like the naturalist, draw the line somewhere in each diverging direction. He must include all the 'Common Words' of literature and conversation, and such of the scientific, technical, slang, dialectal, and foreign words as are passing into common use, and approach the position or standing of 'common words', well knowing that the line he draws will not satisfy all his critics. For to every man the domain of 'common words' widens out in the direction of his own reading, research, business, provincial or foreign residence, and contracts in the direction with which he has no practical connexion: no one man's English is *all* English. The lexicographer must be satisfied to exhibit the greater part of the vocabulary of *each* one, which will be immensely more than the whole vocabulary of *any* one. [11]

This can hardly be challenged. No printed dictionary can possibly satisfy all the people who might conceivably want to use it, although one can imagine a computer-based dictionary which might be able to get considerably closer to the ideal. Even then, however, the information would have to be fed into the computer by human beings, and there is no reason to suppose that people supplying the computer with words, definitions, etymologies and all the rest would have fewer idiosyncrasies, blind spots or prejudices than a research worker for a conventional book-type dictionary. The limitations of size and price would not, however, be of the same importance, and the problem of specialist dictionaries could be solved much more easily and cheaply. Slang dictionaries, science dictionaries, dictionaries of American or Australian English are merely publishing devices. But, even if computer dictionaries were to become practicable and popular, there is little cause for confidence that the information they could provide to a subscriber would be of a superior quality to what is available today. The principal weakness of dictionaries as we know them is that they fail to give adequate guidance as to the occasions on which particular words can and cannot be used, and to the kinds of people to whom they naturally and easily belong. Paradoxically, in order to make full use of a dictionary, one already has to have a good knowledge of the language and of the national cultures and sub-cultures. Dictionaries are to be interpreted, as well as to interpret, and the finer shades of usage of which one must be aware if social disaster is to be avoided are only rarely to be learnt from a dictionary. What dictionary, book or computer would be able, for example, to tell an enquirer that one should not greet the editor of *The Times,* at least at a first meeting, by saying 'Good morning, my dear hack', that British people do not 'hunt' pheasants, and that to look ovine is not normally a synonym for looking sheepish.

It has been said that the dictionary-maker's job is 'not to criticise words, but to collect and explain them'.[12] In practice, however, the three functions cannot be separated. If one assumes that 'criticise' means 'analyse and evaluate', not 'find fault with', it is an inevitable and desirable part of the work that goes into preparing a dictionary. To decide what a word means, what weight it carries, its range of users is surely to criticise it. To think carefully about a word amounts to criticism, and there must be few general words – technical terms are another matter – to which one has no attitude. Most of what Murray called 'common words' have associations of some kind for us and these associations are a powerful factor in conditioning our assessment of them. Words are 'low' for us because we have heard 'low' people using

them. If our view of society does not include the division of our
fellow-citizens into low and non-low, we are unlikely to regard
their language in this way. No word is intrinsically 'low', although
some may offend us aesthetically. It can only be, if we think this
way, the users who are low.

Most people speak far more than they read or write, and it is a
curious, if understandable, feature of dictionaries, certainly from
Johnson onwards, that they rely for their evidence almost entirely
on the printed word. There is the famous story of the lexicographer who wrote to a language journal in the early 1960s
in order to thank the editor for publishing a certain article. His
reason for doing this was that the article in question contained a
word he had been wanting for some time to include in his
dictionary. He knew the word perfectly well, but he had felt
unable to use it until he had discovered it in print.

This point of view, although absurd, made more sense fifty or a
hundred years ago than it does today, mainly because the prestige
of print was much higher then than it is now. What was written
and read had a superior status to what was spoken and heard.
This interesting snobbery had a number of important consequences. Because the written word represented language on
a higher level, certain kinds of expression could not be written
down They would befoul the page and demean the person who
committed the act. But because they were not written down,
there was no evidence that they existed. They were non-words,
primitive forms of communication roughly equivalent to the
grunting of a pig or the cry of a baby. It was hardly possible, even
for the most extreme pedant, to deny the fact of human
conversation, but what people said in the course of their daily
lives became respectable and interesting only after it had been
processed by someone skilled in the art of writing. Speech which
had been heard by a novelist or dramatist, in the course of going
about his daily business, and then regurgitated on to the printed
page, after having been appropriately stylised, refined and
generally made suitable for public consumption, was of quite a
different order. It had become dialogue, and literary dialogue,
unlike raw speech, could be noticed and commented on without
any loss of respectability.

So Dr Murray, like Dr Johnson before him, confined his
attentions to what had been published. The small army of men
and women who collected examples to be used in the compilation

of *The Oxford English Dictionary* were directed towards books, periodicals and newspapers, not towards railway compartment conversations, or to public bar and teatime chatter. There were sound practical reasons for this: it was not entirely a matter of prejudice in favour of the written word. One reason was the problem of accurate recording. The *OED* could not expect its staff to be competent shorthand writers and, even if they had been, it is doubtful if Victorian England would have taken kindly to having their public or private conversations taken down by strangers with notebooks. But, without shorthand, how could these word-collectors have obtained the kind of material their employers would have demanded – full verbal context of the word, which meant a sentence at least; the place and occasion; and the name of the person whose words were being jotted down. One has to imagine something truly impossible, a respectable clergyman, anxious to meet the commitment to his editor in a meticulous, scholarly fashion, saying to a total stranger in a public place, 'Excuse me, I'm from *The Oxford English Dictionary*, and I've just written down something you've said. Could I have your name, age and address, please?' Dr Murray would hardly have settled for less, because what he would have been demanding was the speech equivalent of:

Adverse ... 1858. Ld. St. Leonards *Handy Bk. Prop. Law* XXIII 177. What I may call adverse possession, which is now a possession by a person not the owner during a certain number of years without acknowledgement of the right of the real owner, and yet not necessarily in open defiance of him.

To have reported 'I heard a man refer to his teeth as his "dinner set" on Clapham Junction Station on 11 June 1888' would have been considered unscholarly and inadequate. It would not have met the *Dictionary*'s strict requirements. With printed sources, on the other hand, everyone knew exactly where he was and so, from beginning to end, the research for *The Oxford English Dictionary* was a library job. The four *Supplements* to *The Dictionary*, prepared during the past twenty years, have been worked on in exactly the same way and so, more unexpectedly and strangely, was Eric Partridge's indispensable *Dictionary of Slang and Unconventional English*, first published in 1937. In gathering his material, Partridge drew on a considerable number of previous dictionaries and glossaries, in addition to his own *ad hoc* reading, but at no point does he record something as being merely heard. It has always been read.

Theoretically, the situation facing a dictionary-maker today should be very different. We have tape-recorders, radio and television interviewers have accustomed the public to being asked about anything at any time, and there are huge libraries of recorded speech of all kinds. We ought not to be as dependent on printed material as we were in Victorian times, or even in the 1930s and 1940s, but things have not turned out quite that way. Recorded archives are in fact extraordinarily, infuriatingly difficult to use, partly because the organisations responsible for them are not anxious to offer facilities to students and researchers – staff is always short, budgets are small and playback facilities, especially for film and videotape, are expensive – and partly because listening to and sifting recordings of any kind is an extremely time-consuming business. As anyone who has had to use microfilm and microfiche readers knows all to well, reading books, periodicals and even manuscripts is much quicker and much less tiring. Progress is not always everything it seems. Some day, perhaps, money and methods will be found to allow these great quantities of recorded speech to be used and analysed, instead of just accumulated. But that time is not yet.

But we are, even so, not in quite the same situation as Dr Murray and his colleagues. Most important, our attitude to the spoken word has changed radically during the past thirty or so years. There is no longer the same high regard for print and writing that there once was. This shows itself in many ways. People read less and write worse than they did before the Second World War. They can get by with little more than a nodding acquaintance with these skills. If they want to communicate with their friends and relations or carry out routine business trans-actions, they can telephone or drive. If they want entertainment or information, television and radio are at their disposal.

We therefore have a culture which is largely based on talk, pictures, symbols and statistics. What most people read has to be very close to a transcription of the spoken word. The syntax may be better and the sentences more complete, but the traditional distinction between spoken English and written English has largely disappeared. In broadcast interviews and phone-in pro-grammes, people of all ages are far more confident in expressing themselves than they were in the 1940s. They no longer feel themselves to be members of the silent majority, ashamed of their lack of education and polish or of having the wrong accent. When they write to magazines, they usually do so in their ordinary workaday language, and the editor prints their letters pretty well as they arrive, although the spelling and punctuation may possibly be cleaned up a little.

As a result, the printed record of current speech is far more abundant today than it was when Dr Murray and his colleagues set to work. When Johnson was preparing his *Dictionary* there was virtually no such record at all. Oddly, one type of printed documentation was almost ignored by *The Oxford English Dictionary* group of researchers. The Victorian period was characterised by a remarkable growth of official reports by such specially appointed bodies as Royal Commissions and Parliamentary Committees. For these, evidence was often collected from the kind of people who would never have written anything – factory workers, children in mills and mines, women revealing the facts about the houses they lived in, victims of accidents – and what they said was taken down in shorthand, professionally transcribed and, with the hesitations and repetitions removed and regional and class pronunciations made to conform to standard English spellings, eventually published. The voices of the man, woman and child in the nineteenth-century street have occasionally been preserved for posterity in this way and, both for the social and the linguistic historican, such a record is of immense value.

It is a matter for argument as to how far novelists and playwrights, whether now or in the eighteenth and nineteenth centuries, are a reliable source of information about the speech of their time. They may echo it, but do they reproduce it with anything approaching accuracy? Since all the people who represented their raw material are long dead, it is impossible to be sure. In general, works of fiction need to be used with great caution as sources of linguistic information. We may indeed be impressed by what appears to be 'realistic' or 'convincing' dialogue, but that proves nothing more than the fact that the author is a skilful writer of fiction, a person who understands his craft. Slabs of crude conversation, printed as heard, are quite likely to be remarkably 'unconvincing'. Selection, compression and, above all, styling are required in order to achieve the miracle of sounding like real life. It would be highly dangerous to suppose that all or any mid-Victorian man-servants talked like Sam Weller or that there were archdeacons like Trollope's Archdeacon Grantley. What counts is the flavour and individuality of these characters. The dialect should not be taken to represent the scientific observation and recording of contemporary speech.

All that can safely be said, from a dictionary point of view, is that Shelagh Delaney, for example, knew and used certain words when *A Taste of Honey* was first produced in 1958, or that an observable range of expressions was at Thomas Hardy's disposal in 1878, when *The Return of the Native* was published. But what we can quarry out of the play or the novel is no evidence that either Shelagh Delaney or Thomas Hardy themselves, or the 'real-life' version of any of their characters would have actually spoken like this. All we can say with reasonable certainty is that the words were around at the time, that the writer was satisfied with using them in a particular context and that his readers or audience were prepared to accept the dialogue as it was presented to them. Everything else is supposition.

The only material a dictionary-maker can trust is what some one writes or speaks on his own behalf, in his own person, and this is as true today as it was in the days of Johnson or Murray. *Hansard* tells us, minus the accent, the pauses and intonation, what Members of Parliament actually said. *Kilvert's Diary* gives us the personal style and choice of words of the Rev. Francis Kilvert; *Laughter in the Next Room* is Osbert Sitwell as he wished to present himself to the world. And, on a slightly different level, an article in, say, the *Melody Maker* is both its author and the paper. Individual words from the following passage are acceptable, reasonably reliable dictionary evidence from the pop-music world of the early 1980s.

There's life in there – a lot of big noise and not all of it pleasant, spiky, angular guitars jabbering and brawling and filled with enough energy to light a whole town.

Dickie Henderson and Murray Slade are the guitars responsible for this cockpit of sound, flashing their plumes, pecking and squawking in an insane dervish dance, as if every performance could be their last.

It's an exhilarating show, drenched with blood and feathers, the pair egged on continuously by drummer Russell Burn, denting cowbells and kit to death, and bassist Graham Main, riffing until his fingerpads are torn.

Inevitably, perhaps, the stamina begins to run down and by the time they've begun to work their way through side two they're staggering around with what sounds like a late Sixties blues boom riff and then engaging in medieval primitivism which quickly loses its initial charm. [13]

The *Melody Maker* is essential reading, digging and sifting for anyone who is trying to understand the culture of our time. It has had an exceptionally long career – the first issue was in 1926 – and the musical world it has done its best to publicise and interpret has moved from the palais de danse and negro jazz of the 1920s to the punk rock of the 1980s. Its circulation has risen from a gentle 20,000 to an aggressive and influential quarter of a million. More important, it has shifted its cultural position. From being a small-scale hobby magazine, no different in character from one devoted to gardening or cycling, it has steadily edged its way towards the centre of a youth culture, the size and energy of which was never dreamt of in the 1930s and 1940s. It would hardly be an exaggeration to say that it *is* the new culture: a high proportion of people in their teens and twenties find it easy to identify themselves with its assumptions, its folk heroes, its values, its gamut of interests and its idiom.

Melody Maker is not, of course, the sole occupant of this central ground. *New Musical Express* in Britain and *Rolling Stone* in America do exactly the same. They have become general magazines, with a strong musical emphasis, publications which reflect and form the opinions of the young and the not-so-young, over a wide range of activities. There are many who would object to the term, but they are, in fact, a powerful educational force, and they are required reading for anyone wishing to be well informed about contemporary music.

In saying this, one does not have to pretend that every reader of *Melody Maker* would talk exactly like the passage quoted above. But what this particular journalist wrote would be immediately recognised as being part of the readers' world, the world which has meaning for them. And as they grow up, they carry what we might call *Melody Maker* values and style with them, somewhat less extreme perhaps, but clearly recognisable as not being those of the *Spectator* or even *New Society*. And they feel themselves under no obligation to apologise for these values and interests. They see them as real and valid, as a framework on which to build their lives.

This is a situation which would have appeared absurd, wrong-headed, and indeed impossible to Johnson or Murray, both of whom lived in a world which was regulated by the tastes and opinions of adults, not adolescents. There is no doubt that a great many older people today strongly resent the power which teen-agers have to influence both the national and international environment. A world ruled by teenagers, not unnaturally, does not appeal to them, and it is, indeed, not a particularly en-couraging prospect. Especially, perhaps, they dislike the fact that teenagers speak another kind of language, using a considerable number of expressions which they themselves find either incom-prehensible or repulsive. Disrespect for one's elders and for all they stand for is nothing new as a temporary phase of growing up. What is different and possibly disturbing about the new teenage culture, and the various movements associated with it, is its power and its confidence and its willingness to accept continuous, rapid change as good in itself.

In circumstances such as this, the compilation of anything approaching a reliable, comprehensive dictionary has become almost impossibly difficult. For the task to be practicable and worthwhile, the language has to be persuaded to stand still long enough to be observed and charted. A certain amount of change is admissible, but if change undermines stability, the dictionary-maker has no solid ground on which to build. One could put this another way by saying that to many young people today a dictionary, like any other book between hard covers, is a hostile, provocative object. It is authoritarian, and has too much respect for what is stable and unchanging. It is something created by the Establishment in order to make it easier to assert and maintain its authority, a book of rules, a code of conduct, a straitjacket. There are those who hold the same opinion of standardised spelling and punctuation, and who make a special point of following their own whims and inclinations in these matters, as public evidence of their right to exist as free men. At a conference a year or two ago, I heard one young woman say, 'All dictionaries are fascist', which would have puzzled and shocked Dr Murray considerably, had 'fascist' and its implications been known to him. She might equally well have said, of course, 'All dictionaries are élitist' or 'All dictionaries are sexist'. The point would have been the same. Dictionaries, to her, represented the enemy.

This, when one thinks about it carefully, is a revolutionary attitude. For nearly four centuries, dictionary-makers, like grammarians, have believed they were fulfilling a useful social purpose by helping to regularise spelling and pronunciation, enlarge understanding and assist discrimination. They have said this explicitly and the public, always unsure of itself, has, on the whole, been grateful for their efforts. To a greater or lesser extent, depending on the period and the dictionary, every general dictionary has been a manual of etiquette. It has hinted or said plainly that certain things are done and certain things are not done by people with any claim to civilised behaviour and good manners. 'Taboo', 'slang', 'colloquial' and the rest are essentially warning lights, for the guidance of people who care about such matters.

But suppose they do not care? Suppose these well-meant warning words are meaningless to them? We have reached a point in our society where this is certainly and sadly the case. There are many of our fellow-citizens who do seem to hold precisely this view, after more than a century of compulsory education. They object as strongly to being told how to speak as how to dress, eat or work. Verbal anarchy is merely a reflection of social and political anarchy.

As I have said earlier, for many young people the written word is highly suspect, because it implies permanence, and permanence is both threatening and terrifying. So one must instinctively fight against it wherever it raises its head – having a career or a permanent job is bad, because it suggests permanence; owning a house is bad, for the same reason; having a collection of books or records is bad; having a stock of food is bad. Everything and everyone should be regarded as expendable, replaceable at any time by something different and better suited to one's current mood. To live from day to day is mark of true virtue, a badge of democracy.

Faced with this attitude, what should and can a dictionary do? How does it fit into such a society? What can its philosophy be? The most obvious solution, of course, is to pretend that the situation does not exist, to blot it out of one's mind as something too absurd and unimportant to waste one's time on. It would be easy enough to do this, if people and their habits were not the raw material of the dictionary. After all, *haute couture* does not stop making expensive clothes, simply because most people cannot afford them, and Rolls-Royce unashamedly continues to make extremely high-priced cars for what must inevitably be a very small market. The editor and publisher of a dictionary could, in theory, adopt the same standpoint. They could say that they are working for sensible, serious-minded people, not for irresponsible idiots, and that it is a matter of absolutely no consequence to them if someone is so foolish as to get up at meetings and say, 'Dictionaries are fascist'.

But it does, in fact, matter very much, because the dictionaries-are-fascist attitude is helping, on the one hand, to make the English language much more volatile, and on the other to split it up into opposing social compartments, friendly territory and hostile territory, our words and their words, the English of the young and free, the English of those who love and respect their chains. To try to get as many 'new' words and meanings as possible into one's dictionary is a largely futile exercise, partly because one is going to fall further and further behind chasing language which is changing faster and more radically each year, partly because the ethical basis of what one is doing is unsound – English belongs as much to the poor as to the rich and to layabouts as much as to company chairmen – and partly because the enemies of authority are in possession of a weapon against which there is no defence. Let us call this secret weapon the grandmother's-old-fur-coat syndrome. It can be quite simply explained. For a number of years, many girls have chosen to wear a fur coat which originally belonged to their grandmother or, less probably, to their mother. They would never have considered buying a fur coat for themselves, even if they had happened to have the money: a fur coat, bought new and of fashionable design, would be totally uncharacteristic of their lifestyle and philosophy. It would represent conspicuous expenditure, snobbery and an indifference to the sufferings of animals, all of which are likely to be repulsive to a member of the new generation. But, paradoxically, one can show one's revulsion, one's difference from one's parents, best by wearing the coat, not by not wearing it. Such a person is saying, in effect, 'Look at me. You know the kind of person I am and the kind of ideas and ideals I stand for. For me to wear a coat like this is the same as putting a Dior dress and a diamond necklace on a bonfire guy. You couldn't possibly identify the coat with me, any more than you could the dress and the diamonds with the guy. We both know we look ridiculous, and that is precisely the point. The guy is rubbishing the dress, and I am rubbishing the fur coat. How foolish the original owners were, how enormous is the contrast between me and them. I am wearing this coat in inverted commas and I know you are intelligent enough to notice what I am doing.'

This is exactly what the anti-Establishment, anti-authority generations have been doing with the English language for thirty years or more. They have taken over the language of the previous 'straight' decades and poked gentle fun at it, by placing words and phrases within invisible inverted commas, of which only they and a small body of sympathisers and initiates are aware. The lexicographers, with or without their computers, can do nothing about it. Their entry for the word 'chap' will provide no clue to the fact that a large number of English people habitually use it in inverted commas. The inverted commas are, in fact, the secret weapon. We shall examine the phenomenon more closely in the next chapter.

It is most unwise for a dictionary-maker to offer more than he can deliver. The preface to every new dictionary published during the past half-century, when the business has become steadily more competitive, contains some most perilous statements. Consider, for example, *Collins English Dictionary*, which appeared in 1979. In his foreword, the publisher drew attention to the original research which had gone into the publication, to its distinguished team of experts and advisers and, of course, to the number of words and references which were supplied. He went on: 'We thought it was essential that the dictionary should cover all the spoken and written English that is likely to be required by any but the most highly specialised users'.[14] After 'specialised', he might have inserted 'uncontroversial', because it is quite obvious that what Collins have produced is an excellent dictionary of the traditional kind, a dictionary for crossword-solvers, self-improvers, and etiquette-hunters. So, in the list of advisers, there are experts on religious terms, but not on hippy language, on cards and dancing, but not on pop music, on psychology and anthropology, but not on drugs or homosexuality.

'For the first time in a major dictionary of this kind', says the foreword, with understandable pride, 'computer technology has been used from the inception of the work. This has made it possible to survey every field of human activity subject by subject, defining technical as well as everyday vocabulary in an exceptionally short time.'[15] It is therefore interesting to notice that, of the 2000-odd words and senses in the glossary of British teenage English, which I have prepared, single-handed and computerless, for my own guidance and reference, about a quarter are not to be found in Collins at all. What the moral is, I do not know, since I make no claim whatever to be a lexicographer.

CHAPTER FIVE
Wrong-footing the Enemy

The natives of the Channel Islands play a very subtle and skilful game with visitors. Jersey, Guernsey and the rest enjoy a sub-stratum of Norman-French culture, so that they abound with place names, street names, personal names and shop names which look French. But, for those not in the know, it is impossible to forecast with any accuracy how these words should be pro-nounced. There are three possibilities – French, English and a strange form of bastardised French which bears roughly the same relation to the French of Paris, or even Caen, as Cockney does to standard English – and whichever the innocent visitor chooses is almost certain to be wrong. He has been put gently but unmistak-ably in his place, wrong-footed. Even after years of residence, he will continue to make mistakes. Unerringly correct pronunciation in the Channel Islands is an instinct one has to be born with. The parallel with upper-class English is very close.

But wrong-footing is by no means only a matter of pronuncia-tion. It can equally well involve one's choice of words, stressing, intonation and sentence patterns. What, in the previous chapter, was called the grandmother's-old-fur-coat syndrome is a powerful and widespread method which one generation and cultural group uses in order to wrong-foot another. In order to illustrate how the process works – and it has been an extremely important aspect of the Teenage Revolution – I have chosen twenty-one words, which are presented here, not as a mini-dictionary, but as a collection of case-histories of linguistic takeover and linguistic misunder-standing, set out for convenience in alphabetical order. I have deliberately excluded words and expressions which belong pri-marily to black culture, since these fit more usefully into the next chapter.

Amazing   There is, of course, nothing new or intrinsically puzzling about this word. People of all ages, social classes and educational backgrounds use it and have done for generations. But in the late 1950s it became a great favourite among teenagers, backed up by the ad-men, and was one of *the* superlatives of the 1960s and 1970s. It is noticeably less in vogue with this age-group now than it was five years ago, and to continue to use it as if it were still a high-fashion word is to confess one's age and out-of-date habits.

But, and this is the important point, it was always difficult, even at the height of the word's popularity, to be sure whether young people were using it straight or with a degree of irony, in inverted commas, whether they were mocking the advertisers and publicity men who were writing for them. The difference could perhaps be expressed in this way. When *International Times* wrote, 'The charity could organise amazing concerts',[1] it was consciously and perhaps cynically employing a cliché. These pop concerts were not really outstanding or even spectacular. They were simply well promoted and successful, and 'amazing' was no more than a typical example of publicity puff. But if a teenager who attended the concert said afterwards that it had been 'amazing', he or she would almost certainly have been using the word in a slightly but significantly different way, not least because he was speaking, not writing. The tone of voice would have contained a faint, possibly more than faint, quotation element.

Band   Used in the sense of 'a musical combination', 'band' has moved in and out of fashion during the past forty years in a most bewildering manner. Until the early 1950s, 'band' was the normal word so far as popular music was concerned. Then, with pop music replacing popular music, 'group' took over. Pop and rock music was always played by 'groups', not 'bands', partly because 'band' seemed altogether too grand and pretentious for three or four people playing together – a 'band' traditionally had a conductor and its members were likely to wear dinner jackets or some other kind of uniform – and partly because 'group' was felt to be a better word to describe the informal, democratic, closely-knit character of the performers. There was also the important distinction between the old-fashioned 'band', whose members could read music, and the 'group', none of whom could usually read a note.

From the early 1970s onwards, 'band' came back into the main stream again. Older people, reared on 'dance bands' and 'military bands', had never stopped using it, and had often made themselves figures of fun by referring to 'groups' as 'bands'. Now, however, 'band' because a perfectly respectable and normal term for small run-of-the-mill pop and rock groups, although quite frequently, perhaps usually, it was not used entirely seriously by insiders and tended to have a marked flavour of pastiche about it. The word was detached from the organised, musically literate musicians, to whom it properly belonged, and transferred, as a piece of verbal fancy-dress, to the 'groups', whom hostile observers felt made noises rather than music. The smile in the voice, which was obvious to initiates, when a 'group' was dignified by being called a 'band', tended to pass unnoticed by those who felt that such a perverse habit simply devalued the currency and that to call a modern collection of musical mountebanks by a previously honourable title amounted to something close to blasphemy.

Black   'Black', like 'coloured', is a most difficult word to use in Britain today, and has been for thirty years or more, although the situation is by no means the same now as in the 1950s. To begin with, black people have been sacred figures to the middle-class British young for more than a full generation, and to criticise them in any way or to laugh at them has been the equivalent of blasphemy or jokes about bishops in High Victorian England. This attitude has represented a gulf between the generations. Those in Britain who reached adulthood before the late 1940s, whatever their social class, certainly showed no particular respect for black people and, even today, a considerable proportion of our working-class young people probably feel the same way.

In the 1960s, for a white person to call a negro 'black' was considered insulting by many young whites and by the blacks themselves, although Americans of both skin colours were using the term quite freely by then. During the 1970s it became acceptable and eventually more respectable here to use the adjective 'black', instead of 'coloured', although the noun was still felt to be offensive, and 'black people' was preferred. There is a close parallel with 'Jews' and 'Jewish people'.

After twenty years of the Black Rights movement in America, and equivalent activity in Britain, 'black' is now used proudly and aggressively by black people and only slightly more diffidently by whites, especially young whites. 'Coloured' has been largely abandoned, except by the police, some members of the working class, especially women and girls, and upper-middle-class ladies getting on in years.

It is interesting to note that it became normal to say 'black' earlier among pop musicians than in any other social group, almost certainly because those most closely connected with the pop world brought the current American usage to Britain. Among teenagers today the use of 'black', rather than 'coloured', and vice versa seems to be determined largely by social class and to a rather lesser extent by sex. In 1979, 'I've been going out with my boyfriend for two months now. But the trouble is he's coloured'[2] could hardly have been written by a middle-class girl, except perhaps with the verbal equivalent of a gentle smile, and 'I've been going out with my girlfriend for two months now. But the trouble is she's coloured' would have been quite impossible at this date for a working-class boy.

To distinguish the presence or absence of mental inverted commas around 'coloured' requires much experience and well-developed sensitivity to English social thinking and habits, especially in those cases where teenagers are poking fun at the attitudes of their parents.

Boutique   Until the early 1960s, a 'boutique' was an exclusive, expensive small shop selling women's clothes and accessories. It was often run as a profitable sideline by one of the *haute couture* houses. Towards the end of the decade a very different kind of boutique emerged, a noisy, crowded Carnaby Street type of shop, selling trendy and often cheap clothes to the young of both sexes. This meaning has now disappeared, and the word is now used entirely in its original up-market sense, which it had never lost among those for whom high fashion and high prices had always been synonymous. The occasional ironical use of 'boutique' to describe a youth-attire shop which is anything but up-market is liable to cause confusion and bewilderment among those older people whose inclination is to take words at their face value.

'Around the boutiques with Sam'[3] and 'Are you wearing the most way-out clothes you could find in the boutique?'[4] represent the original teenage take-over of a word previously considered the rightful monopoly of Christian Dior, Hardy Amies and the rest of the first league.

Caff   A British, basically working-class abbreviation of 'café', borrowed in America and Australia only by those who are using it consciously and slightly mockingly as a foreign word. In Britain itself it has for many years been considered distinctly uneducated, if not low, without being associated with any particular age-group, but for the past thirty years it has also been used half-seriously by young people with a middle-class background who are anxious to provide evidence of their essential classlessness or, alternatively, of their solidarity with their working-class contemporaries. But there is usually no great difficulty in distinguishing those to whom 'caff' comes naturally from those for whom it represents a revolt against the real or imagined class-consciousness of their 'café' parents.

Chap   'Chap', meaning 'man', is traditionally a middle-to-upper-class word. It is still used straight and without affectation by both sexes within these sections of society. From the 1950s onwards, however, it has become part of the vocabulary of working-class boys and girls, and of journalists of the *Private Eye* type, but with overtones which were never in the minds of the original users.

The working-class take-over of the word has involved a slight element of ridicule, of public-school mateyness and team spirit. All in all, the descent of 'chap' down the social scale represents a very fine example of the grandmother's-old-fur-coat syndrome but, for women and girls below the upper middle class it has come to be used in quite a different way, as a much-favoured neutral synonym for 'man' which, for interesting reasons, is avoided as much as possible. On this, see also FELLOW.

Examples abound of the 'So watch it, chaps'[5] and 'This is spiffing wheeze music. Great ideas, chaps'[6] type.

Charming   This youth-expression, current in the 1960s, is still flourishing today. Always used on its own and as an exclamation, it has to be uttered with crushing irony, in order to damn something which is considered the exact opposite of charming.

'Charming! He really had me worried there'[7] gives the typical

flavour. Used in this sense, 'charming!' functions as a replacement
for 'how nice', which tended, however, to belong rather further
up the social scale. It is interesting to notice that those for whom
'charming!' forms a regular part of the vocabulary are more likely
to be female than male and to confine themselves to using the
word ironically and as an exclamation. They would never say, for
instance, that a person was charming. For the young, 'charming'
cannot be a term of praise.

Chum   This is a most difficult word for many English people
and a nearly impossible one for foreigners. Until the early or
mid-1960s it continued to be used in its old warm, approving
sense of 'good friend, constant companion'. This meaning does
still continue, but mainly among older women. Nowadays,
however, 'chum' is usually found as a pejorative. With teenagers,
the translation often has to be 'unpleasant friend, crony', as in
'She makes fun of you from across the road, with her gang of
chums'[8] and with rather older people, especially journalists, who
have emerged from approximately the same sub-culture, 'chum'
is often almost a synonym for 'accomplice', especially in unscrupulous or underhand business deals. One distinguishes this
meaning in, for example, 'The Grocer, an old sailing chum of
Marley boss, Owen Aisher',[9] and in 'fast-moving committee-work
with Arnold Wesker and chums'.[10]

It would probably be accurate to say that, given the results of
the take-over of 'chum' by the youth–pop movements of twenty
years ago, the word is now best avoided. In any given situation,
one can never be sure how seriously it is being used and with
precisely what connotation. This may well be the most likely
explanation, other than a mere shift of fashion, for why it has
gone out of favour with teenagers. The verb, meaning 'to be
friends with someone', has gone the same way.

Clobber   During the past hundred years, this word, meaning
'clothes', has passed from one sub-culture to another in a most
interesting, if bewildering, way. It was common among Jewish
people, especially in London, and among Gentile Cockneys from
the mid-nineteenth century onwards and it has been in general
use in Australia during the present century. It is what one might
call a chameleon type of word. According to its context, it looks
and feels characteristically and convincingly Jewish, Cockney or

Australian. It was a much-used public-school word in the 1930s and the Teenage Revolutionaries swallowed it up eagerly in the 1950s and 1960s, only to reject it equally strongly in the 1970s, when it was replaced by 'gear'. In the sense of 'clothes', it now has a distinctly upper-class, boarding-school image.

During its heyday as a favourite teenage word, however, it was much used by somewhat older people as a useful portmanteau expression for 'possessions, luggage', as in 'I'll give you a hand with all your clobber',[11] and with no particular class associations. This meaning is now very dated. The verb, 'to clobber', has shown much greater stamina in recent years. Meaning 'to hit', it is common in America, where the noun has never taken the public's fancy. In Britain, it is used more or less equally by all age-groups, but it is felt to be distinctly middle- and upper-class and when people with a working-class background use it, there is usually more than a touch of quotation in their voice.

There is no restriction on what may be clobbered. Both a person and an object may receive this treatment. 'When in doubt, clobber the car',[12] advised the *Guardian* a few years ago.

Fab, fabulous   The two words share the same dictionary definition, 'wonderful, marvellous', and they were both in vogue during the 1960s, but they were by no means interchangeable. 'Fabulous' was probably the most widely used superlative of the decade. Those who belonged to the theatre world and its fringes used it in every other sentence – actresses had a way of over-stressing the first syllable which was all too easy to caricature, the debby level of British society loved it, and journalists and advertisers made much of it. The age-range of its users stretched from 13 or 14 at the bottom end to a gallant 40 at the top, with women and girls slightly, but only slightly, in the majority. The ordinary run of boys tended to play it down slightly by prefacing it with words like 'pretty'. If one described something as 'pretty fabulous', one could remain firmly and unmistakably male and yet be in the fashion.

'Fab', on the other hand, was rarely used in speech by anyone but teenagers and throughout its very short career in the mid-1960s it remained solidly British. Its rise coincided with that of the Beatles, 'the Fab Four', who were alleged to use it, although there is little reliable evidence that they in fact did. It was used as an exclamation, as well as an adjective.

It lingered on with journalists catering for teenagers longer than among teenagers themselves. Journalists, like novelists, take a long time to catch up with fashions in speech and not infrequently find themselves in the unenviable position of acting as impresario to habits that are actually dead or dying. In this particular instance, however, the journalists may have been lucky, because there are signs that 'fab' may be staging something of a comeback among a new generation of teenagers. Examples of the revival were to be found in 1979 – 'I think Lewis Collins is absolutely fab and I'd like to join his fan club'[13] – and they have become more numerous since. But it is still too early to be sure.

Fella, fellow   Many, perhaps most, adults do not realise the important difference which is reflected by the two spellings. Broadly speaking, 'fellow' is used by anyone, male or female, of any age, while 'fella', sometimes spelt 'fellah', nowadays belongs to girls and young women exclusively. This was not the situation before the 1950s. From about 1870 onwards, 'fella' and 'fellah' – spellings which reflected the pronunciation – were looked on by most people as upper-class and affected, while 'feller' verged on the low. There may have been some influence, so far as the 'fella'/'fellah' pronunciation was concerned, with 'fellah', an Egyptian peasant. The idea of calling a fellow-officer a 'fellah' must have seemed very funny to members of the British army in Victorian times.

It is worth noticing that, until the 1950s, only a man would call another man a 'fella'. It was not a form of the word that women, even upper-class women, used, although 'fellow' was very much part of their vocabulary. But, once the Teenage Revolution was under way in Britain, it was mainly girls who took over 'fella' from the officers and gentlemen who had previously had a monopoly of it.

So we find, in magazines aimed at the 18-and-under age-group, 'Last week I met this fella that I've fancied for ages'[14] and 'What with a dishy fella and super job, it's no wonder she's very happy'.[15] 'This fellow that I've fancied for ages' and 'What with a dishy fellow . . .' would have been impossible.

Girlfriend   Until the 1950s, Britain and the English language seem to have got along quite well without 'girlfriend' and 'boyfriend'. One did not, so far as memory serves, feel greatly deprived by the lack of them. One had a 'friend', one had a 'girl' or a 'boy', and it was assumed, one supposes, that, if one had a 'girl', she was friendly. It was not considered necessary to emphasise the point.

But, with the arrival of the permissive society, the situation ceased to be simple. Sexual relationships became less predictable and more complicated and nobody knew quite how to describe anybody any more. A 'girlfriend' could no longer be assumed to be merely a friend who was a girl. She might be, but she might also be the girl with whom one happened to be living at the time. She might not even be a girl. A 'girlfriend' could easily turn out to be a woman of distinctly mature years.

Moreover, it gradually became apparent that homosexuality and lesbianism were far more common than one had ever suspected. So 'boyfriend' and 'girlfriend' were urgently required, as a guarantee that one was heterosexual. In such a climate, a 'friend' could be anything.

'Girlfriend' and 'boyfriend' therefore scored on all counts. They were invaluable omni-purpose terms, covering all possibilities and ensuring the maximum discretion, even if they sounded wordy, clumsy and unBritish, which they undoubtedly were since they were imported from America, where the revolution in teenage behaviour had moved more quickly. Many people whose taste in words had been formed in more innocent days regretted the loss of the old simplicity. 'My girlfriend Paula'[16] would have been just 'my friend Paula' thirty years earlier, and, among educated people, it still is.

For the young themselves, however, 'girlfriend' and 'boyfriend' are strong defences against the inquisitive habits of parents and older people generally. Since they are far from being precise terms, guesses and accusations are very likely to be wrong.

Guy   In the sense of 'man, fellow, chap', the word 'guy' was current in the United States in the 1890s and had established itself in Britain twenty years later. During the subsequent three-quarters of a century its original American flavour has largely, but not completely, disappeared here and it is still true to say that it is used much more frequently and naturally in American English than it is on this side of the Atlantic. In post-Second World War Britain the social pattern of its usage could be summarised approximately as follows. The popular press and especially the pop-music press has gone for it wholeheartedly. Uneducated people favour it more than educated people, but the educated young not infrequently give the impression of using it in faint inverted commas, as if it were not really one of their words and they were amusing themselves with it. Among young people of the working class it is particularly well thought of by women and girls, for whom it provides yet another opportunity to avoid the more crudely biological word, 'man'.

So the *Daily Mirror* describes a pop star as being 'as nice a guy off stage as he is on it',[17] which *The Times* and the *Daily Telegraph* certainly would not, *Jackie*, whose survival depends on the goodwill of working-class teenage girls, gives advice on 'how to capture the ski-instructor, or any other guy you fancy',[18] and *New Musical Express* refers to 'this guy, Presley'.[19] *My Guy* could hardly fail to promote its own name, and on its problem page we are told, not surprisingly, that 'what is awful is sleeping with a guy just for the sake of it'.[20] In all these examples, the word is used straight and without the irony which would be likely to be present on more cultivated levels.

Hubby This cosy abbreviation of 'husband' was in general British, but not American, use from the late seventeenth century until the outbreak of the Second World War. During the latter part of this long and honourable career – that is, between the wars – it always had a markedly lower middle-class flavour. It was firmly and absolutely non-U.

Since about 1950 it has been used, especially by the younger and trendier journalists, in a rather patronising way, emphasising the more trivial and often hen-pecked aspects of domestic life, and nearly always from the point of view of an observer – that is, in the third person. The pre-war first- and second-person usage – 'My hubby says', 'What does your hubby think?' – has almost disappeared, and what we now have is 'hubby strumming a little guitar'[21] and 'hubby sitting with eyeballs glued to the little screen'.[22]

Few, if any, of the pre-war generations for whom 'hubby' was part of ordinary conversation are likely to be readers of *New Musical Express* or *Private Eye*. If they were, they would probably be comforted and encouraged to find one of their old friends still in use and in print, without realising the change of attitude which had taken place without their knowing about it.

Kid Until the post-war revolution turned the English language as well as British society upside down and inside out, 'kid' was a slightly patronising, but not unfriendly, way of referring to a boy or girl under the age of 14, or thereabouts. During the past three decades, however, three distinct meanings have developed.

The first, for those who are not sensitive to subtle linguistic change or who are misled by superficial resemblances, appears no different from the pre-war colloquialism. It is simply 'a child', or so it would seem. But this is not, in fact, so. Nowadays it is perfectly acceptable, in a way it was not forty or fifty years ago, to refer to children as 'kids' even in quite formal contexts, if one is, for example, a teacher, social worker or politician. The use of the word by such people as this implies understanding and familiarity, and the warm-hearted acceptance of the 'kids' by the speaker.

But 'kid' can also mean 'a young person, a teenager'. When the word is used in this sense by teenagers themselves, the upper age-limit is higher than when older people use it. It can be 18, 19 or even more. During the 1950s and 1960s it was part of the hippy and near-hippy vocabulary and emphasised group identity and solidarity. 'The small seaside town was full of warring kids'[23] means that gangs of 16- and 18-year-olds, not children, were fighting one another.

A third meaning, closely linked to the second, is 'supporter, follower, fan'. This is found particularly in the world of football – 'It's not the kids who are letting football down, it's the other way round'[24] – and pop music – 'The kids think we're breaking up'.[25]

The situation is further confused by the fact that the old meaning continues side by side with the new ones. Kids continue to get lost, eat sweets and generally make a nuisance of themselves as they always did, but, as they pass out of this phase, they become kids of a different kind, brothers and sisters in the forward march of youth.

Lad For a long time, certainly for the whole of the present century, 'lad' has had two meanings. A 'lad' has been a boy and he has also been a member of a team or similarly closely-knit group. During the First World War, for example, officers were accustomed to encourage their men to perform unpleasant tasks, like rushing into a hail of enemy bullets, by shouting 'Come on, lads'. This is a purely British usage, which has not spread to other parts of the English-speaking world.

In recent years 'lads' has acquired, in the plural only, certain sinister overtones which the word did not possess previously. Nowadays, 'the lads' are all too likely to be a gang or mafia preparing to impose its will on society at large, or on some substantial part of it. The shop steward who told a reporter, 'My lads couldn't take any more'[26] was using the word in this sense, with an implied threat that the other side had better give way or else, and there is a far from peaceful and friendly note in '1973–4 will go down as the season that the lads started coming on to the pitch'.[27]

For those such as trade union leaders, whose constant task is to rally the troups behind them, 'lads' has proved a godsend. It can suggest a greater degree of cohesion and unity of purpose than in fact exists. It helps both to define and to cement the group and, for many, it is flattering to be considered one of the 'lads'.

Lady This is a very tricky word indeed to use today. In Britain, working-class females strongly dislike being called 'women', although 'girl' is perfectly acceptable, especially when applied to those well advanced in years. So, to avoid giving offence, it has to be 'tea-lady', 'cleaning-lady', 'checkout-lady' and all the rest. 'Woman' is preferred by the educated section of the middle class, however, and female students are as firmly 'women students' as they were fifty years ago. Among members of this group, 'ladies' is considered a bourgeois vulgarism. 'Lady students' would be impossible.

In the late 1960s, 'lady' began to be used by young Americans as a normal synonym for 'girl, woman', often with affectionate overtones and not at all tongue-in-cheek. It crossed the Atlantic with this attitude around it to become, first, part of the vocabulary of students and the super-hip and then of journalists and certain sections of the younger middle class. At this point, its usage began to coalesce with that of the strangely prudish working class, as outlined above.

There are complications. Upper-middle-class people, who would normally use 'woman' when talking to others of their own class, will often exchange this for 'lady' when the other person in the conversation is working-class or lower-middle-class. And throughout British society a 'lady' becomes a 'woman' when one is annoyed with her or feels she has done something stupid.

Although 'lady' is now nearly universal among young people of all social and educational backgrounds, one does sometimes get the impression that the more intelligent and better-educated are using it somewhat with their tongue in their cheek. But, as with so many of the expressions which have associations with Britain's genteel past, it is extremely difficult to be sure.

Loo   This all-conquering word for 'lavatory' was in very limited and very exclusive upper-class use in the late 1930s. During the 1950s and 1960s it drove its way steadily downwards through the various levels of the middle class and in the 1970s it reached the upper strata of the working class. In the course of its descent it met the equally class-conscious 'toilet' moving equally steadily upwards. These two great euphemisms now seem to have agreed on a very approximate frontier. Loo Land is, broadly speaking, inhabited by families whose children belong to the exam-passing class, and Toilet Land by all the rest. This is much the same as saying that the boundary lies somewhere towards the bottom of the lower middle class, but there are important qualifications to be made to this generalisation. The North of England uses the word 'loo' less than the South does, and women everywhere favour it rather more than men do. The working-class under-21s often speak it in a way which suggests that they consider it to be a piece of upper-class preciousness and that they are making use of the word only in order to laugh at it.

It is to be heard in certain circles in America but very much as a British export and with the same sort of cachet as Scottish knitwear or Wedgwood china.

Mum   In England – the situation in Scotland, Wales and Ireland is rather different – one could probably place a person socially with fair accuracy if one were to study only his or her use of 'mum'. As a generalisation, one could say that it is a term which can be used naturally and easily only between parent and child and that it tends to be avoided in favour of 'mother' by families which belong to the upper and upper middle classes. 'Mummy', however, is fully U.

But this is to oversimplify the situation. A middle-class mother would find it perfectly possible to refer to 'all the mums' waiting for their children outside the local primary school, but would never speak of 'the mums' congregated for the Eton and Harrow match, or for Speech Day at Cheltenham Ladies College. Journalists and headline writers are enthusiastic users of 'mum', partly for its blessed shortness and partly for its warm, sentimental, cosy flavour. To use 'mum' rather than 'mother' is to prove that one's heart beats with the people. It even has to be 'the Queen Mum'.

'If you ask nicely, Mum will help you with any bits you find tricky', suggests *Judy Annual for Girls*.[28] *Judy Annual* is aimed at young girls, not teenagers, and its choice of 'Mum', instead of 'your mother', has a touch of self-consciouness, and is slightly patronising, while at the same time revealing an anxiety to be on familiar terms with its readers. 'Foster mum Jeannette Roberts'[29] provides a different set of clues. As used by certain professionals – journalists writing for women and health visitors are two good examples – 'mum' combines a mildly patronising flavour with a desire to appear democratic and informal, an approach which contains a serious danger of insincerity.

The only way in which to protect oneself against the pitfalls of using 'mum' is to place oneself at a slight distance from the word, either by the tone of one's voice or by planning the context carefully, and that is precisely what a great many young people do. When they say, for example, 'My mum told me', they are apt to use an accent which is not quite their own, and so to hunt both with the hare and with the hounds.

Really As an exclamation, 'really!' with the appropriate pronunciation, was a much-caricatured feature of upper-class speech during most of the first half of the present century. Said in the way it used to be said, it has virtually disappeared. There is no sign whatever that it has been taken up by the postwar generations, anxious to prove that the English language belongs to the whole people and that one is free to pillage and adapt in whichever direction one pleases.

What has happened, however, is that a purely teenage use has been discovered for 'really' as an alternative to 'very much' or, not infrequently, as a meaningless intensive. Used in both these ways, 'really' became an extremely popular feature of teenage speech in the 1960s and remained so until very recently, although it is now showing signs of obsolescence. It was hardly ever used by anyone who had ceased to be a teenager by 1980 and it marks a sharp dividing line between the generations. Many of those who learnt it as teenagers have continued to use it. These include many journalists, who help to keep their youthful speech habits in print if not exactly alive. It is a circular process. The journalists write, 'When I played to Col, he really liked it'[30] and 'The bike is good and I really feel I can put it all together this year'[31] and the teenagers imitate what they read. But it is a process which cannot continue indefinitely.

Super   In the years immediately following the Second World War, 'super!' was a very upper-class exclamation. Pronounced in a characteristically debutante or Guards officer manner, it was easy to caricature and became a rather overdone joke among other sections of the community. As an exclamation, it made very little progress down the social scale, except as a way of poking fun at what was felt to be upper-class snootiness.

Its popularity as an adjective was quite another matter. This was mainly a 1960s vogue among teenagers – 'Here's a super game to play'.[32] 'It's one of the super ideas of the boutique's owner',[33] and so on – but it was fading fast by the 1970s, except in compounds such as 'supergenius', supermod', 'superhero' and 'superstar', many of which came from America. The tedious overemployment of the word, especially by professional publicists, has worn it out and robbed it of much of its appeal. The upper-class 'super' was killed by ridicule and by the decline in prestige of the class which bred it; the 'super' of more ordinary mortals has been forced into retirement by sheer exhaustion.

The list of examples given above could have been extended many times. It illustrates a number of different aspects of the process which I have called 'wrong-footing the enemy', sending him searching in the wrong direction, confusing him, causing him to believe that the facts are other than what they really are. No planned campaign is involved. Things just happen the way they do and each generation and half-generation lives increasingly within its own world of comprehension.

CHAPTER SIX

The Influence of Real and Imaginary Blacks

'The black man, by his presence in the community, made everything possible', wrote Dick Hebdige.[1] It was an interesting observation. Since the large-scale immigration from the West Indies and the Caribbean during the 1940s and 1950s, the attitudes of the British people have undergone a great change. Whether this has been for the better or for the worse, and to what extent the blacks, either as individuals or as a community, have been a major cause is a matter for discussion and, so far, prejudice has prevented this exceedingly important question from being answered with the care and objectivity it deserves. If the introduction of large numbers of people with a different skin colour and a different culture has, over a period of thirty or forty years, so shaken British society that its traditional values and modes of expression no longer exist, especially among the young, then we have been witnessing something comparable to what took place in Russia between 1917 and 1921, something for which 'revolution' can hardly be too strong a word. But Hebdige may conceivably be exaggerating or he may be on the wrong track altogether. In order to be in a position to make up our minds on the point, we need to know what kind of black culture was brought across the Atlantic to Britain, how that culture expressed itself in words and other forms of behaviour, and how the British have reacted to an immigration which was upon them before they began to realise what was happening.

One should begin by establishing certain basic facts. During the twenty years from 1945 to 1965, the peak period of the immigration, black people were coming to Britain at an average rate of about 40,000 a year, which is roughly equivalent to the population of Ashford, Kent, or Stanley, Co. Durham. One could put this more dramatically by saying that every year, for two whole decades, Britain was being required to absorb one medium-sized town wholly populated by blacks. The actual problem was more serious than this, because the new arrivals had a great many children after they reached Britain. It is impossible to determine anything like an accurate figure, because the colour of a new baby's skin is not entered on its birth certificate and nobody maintains a register of black citizens as such, but it is quite possible that by 1981 about one resident of the British Isles in twelve was black. This figure takes no account of the smaller, but by no means inconsiderable, number of immigrants from India and Pakistan who arrived at the same time. Let us say that, at the time of writing in 1982, one British resident in ten over the whole country has a black or brown skin. There is no record of what the proportion may have been before the Second World War, but it was certainly insignificant.

Mere numbers are not everything, however, and something needs to be said about the quality of all these people. Two kinds of generalisation are reasonable. The first concerns the skills and employability of the immigrants, and the second their willingness to adapt to British habits and values. In both of these respects, those who came from the Caribbean and the West Indies have shown themselves very different from those from the Indian sub-continent.

Nearly all of our first generation of black immigrants could be broadly defined as working-class. Very few had any professional skills and very few were involved in what one might call the entrepreneurial occupations, shop-keeping, merchanting, the running of small manufacturing businesses. On the other hand, they had come from countries where unemployment and poverty were rampant and they had seized on emigration as a chance to improve their situation. There was at that time no shortage of jobs in Britain – that is why they had been encouraged to come in the first place – and they found themselves able to enjoy a standard of living which would have been, in most cases, quite unattainable had they remained where they had been born. They had every reason to follow the traditional immigrant pattern and to do their best to conform to British customs and, to their credit, because it cannot have been easy, many of them did so.

For their children, however, the problem has been different.

Some of the boys, and probably a rather higher proportion of the girls, worked hard at school and acquired qualifications and middle-class jobs. A great many others, however, decided that British society had nothing to offer them and that they were doomed to second- and third-class jobs, if indeed they were able to find any work at all. Having come to this conclusion, they gave up whatever attempt they might have made to become an integrated part of Britain and found much greater attractions in the concept of a segregated black British culture, based on the Rastafarian movement. The second generation of blacks in Britain was, paradoxically, more African and less British than the first and, whatever their inclinations may have been, white teenagers found it steadily more difficult to make effective contact with their black contemporaries. Music was no longer the powerful link between the two cultures that it had once been. As a token of this, we can note that *Black Music*, launched at the end of 1973, was aimed specifically at the West Indian market.

With the Indians and Pakistanis, the situation was quite different. The romance of India may have been a reality to those families and generations which had served the Raj, but it meant nothing at all to the British teenagers of the 1950s and 1960s. A great many of them felt that they had a lot in common with the West Indians, but, for all the professed hostility to 'racism', and for all the pretence that skin colour was of no importance, it was rare to find a British boy or girl showing much enthusiasm for Indians or Indian culture. Indians had too many disadvantages to make them acceptable friends and allies – they were hard-working, entrepreneurial, peace-loving and quiet and, so it was imagined, they almost certainly voted Conservative. The blacks were considered to be pleasantly idle, unambitious, anarchic and vaguely left-wing: the Indians and Pakistanis were thrusting, law-abiding and ambitious for both themselves and their children.

All such folk-labels contain a large mythical element, of course, but, so far as human prejudice is concerned, stereotypes, however ill-founded, often, perhaps usually, have a more power-ful effect than reality. To a great extent, people believe what they want to believe. In the case of the blacks, there was a complica-tion which has not received the attention it deserves. Until the 1950s, few British people had ever met more than the occasional negro or Indian, and even now there are many parts of the country where it is rare to see a face that is not white. What they knew about them mostly came from films, books, magazines and hearsay, and even then their views concerned mainly the negroes of the United States. The West Indians, by comparison, had received very little publicity, and there were and still are important cultural differences between the blacks of North America and the blacks of the Caribbean and the West Indies, although the Black Power movement of the past thirty years has helped to develop a feeling of common identity and purpose which did not exist previously.

An impartial observer can hardly fail to note that among young people in postwar Britain the blacks have been romanticised and idealised to an extent which recalls the very similar treatment given to the Russians by the political left. If, as Hebdige suggests, the black section of the community has been so influential in determining the national atmosphere and aspirations of Britain during the past three decades, then it should be emphasised that a large part of this influence has come from imaginary and theoretical blacks, rather than real ones. It is by no means the first time in history that such a thing has happened. The modern admirers of the Greeks and Romans, for instance, would almost certainly have had a profound shock and experienced considerable disillusionment if they had been able to meet their heroes face to face and to talk to them for a week or so. And so with the Russians, the Chinese, the Biblical Hebrews and most of the other great myth-engendering races of history. If one needs to have idols, it is better not to know too much about them.

How, then, does the negro in Western society appear, to himself and to any fair-minded white person who has taken off his rose-tinted spectacles? It is probably most helpful to begin with the negro in the United States, since it is here, outside Africa, that he is to be found in greatest numbers and here that such recent phenomena as Black Awareness, Black Pride and Black Power have developed earliest.

The American negro became urbanised during the last decade of the nineteenth century and the first three of the twentieth. The great migration from country to town 'brought the Negro masses into contact with the quickened pulse of the modern city. There they were faced with a mass of strange experiences which forced them to revise their traditional ways of thinking. The crowded ghetto, unlike the isolated farm, provided a basis for a vigorous group life. A rising standard of living and better educational

opportunities fostered new attitudes of self-respect and independence. In a word, the Negro's urban environment lifted him
to a new plane of consciousness.'[2]

This new world of urban blacks acquired a race capital,
Harlem, which, betwen 1900 and 1920, gradually pushed out the
whites and doubled its numbers. Its population was not drawn
only from the United States. Considerable numbers came from
the West Indies and even from Africa itself, an aspect of black
American society which has usually been overlooked, the
accepted view being that the United States acquired its basic
stock of blacks during the eightcenth and early nineteenth
centuries and that the supply from the African homeland was
then permanently cut off.

But, whether inside or outside the United States, there was a
new interest in negro life and culture among whites after the First
World War. Black art, especially sculpture, in Africa and black
music in America began to attract considerable attention and
admiration, for reasons which are not at all difficult to explain.
The white West had become tired of its sophistication, repres-
sions and inhibitions. The black man stood out in contrast as
a symbol of unspoilt, innocent man, living by his instincts and
emotions, rather than by following the strict rules and patterns of
an industrial society. During the first half of the present century,
this appeal came mostly to educated adults, and particularly to
artists; from the late 1940s onwards, it was much more the
teenager who found in blacks and black culture a set of symbols
of the kind of life he wanted for himself. The black man, he felt,
was free in ways he himself was not.

Among artists, dealers, collectors and art journalists in Europe
and America, interest in the negro was centred on a cult of the
primitive. Primitivism, with its not infrequently absurd idealism
of simpler cultures, is essentially a form of withdrawal from the
complexities and tensions of modern life, a twentieth-century
version of Rousseau and the Noble Savage. The inspiration and
satisfaction of the primitive lies in its preference for instinct to
intellect and in the way in which it allows puritanism to be
brushed aside as irrelevant to human needs and the human
condition. The negro represented, rather than was, the unspoilt
child of nature. He was spontaneous, carefree and – most
important for a country like Britain or America, which was slowly
shaking itself free of Victorianism – sexually uninhibited. Carving

and sculpture in Africa and jazz in the United States were, in the
1920s and 1930s, the best-known and most influential expressions
of Natural Black Man, as the white avant-garde saw him.

But the black man as he actually is, and as he sees himself, is
rather a different person. A great deal of research has been
concerned with this during the past ten years, especially in the
United States, and the general result of it has been, from the
point of view of white people, rather discouraging in the sense
that the possibility of whites and blacks gradually developing a
common culture seems extremely unlikely. 'We asked ourselves
the following basic question', wrote the extremely assiduous and
objective editor of a recent American book on the subject. 'What
do adult black males and females see and value in various
situations that make a difference to the way they behave?'[3] All the
contributors to this symposium, some white, some black, assumed
a black norm that is equally valid with a white norm, not a
deviation from it, and they came to a number of interesting
conclusions.

The first was, on the whole, not at variance with the idea of the
noble, uninhibited black man. Negroes rated the heart above the
head and valued something called 'soul' very highly indeed.
'Soul', a very difficult word to define, means, roughly, 'rapport
with people like oneself, with other blacks; warm, instinctive
understanding'. Whatever a person with 'soul' does is determined
directly and honestly by what his heart tells him. A 'soul' person
never thinks of strategy or tactics, never plots or schemes, is never
devious. His meaning is never in doubt, always provided the other
person has 'soul', too. And since, with very few exceptions, only
black people can possess 'soul', true communication between
blacks and whites is almost impossible.

But, within black culture and the black community, communication is by no means only a matter of words. Body language is
equally important. The way one stands or walks conveys a
message from one black person to another, and so does something
known as 'giving skin', the stylised, ritualistic way in which
one person places his hand against another's. Such a system
of messages is more important to black people than to white,
because black people are communal by nature. They do not
esteem individualism in quite the same way that white people do,
although they have a high opinion of someone who is a good
performer in public.

A person with 'soul' is permitted to say anything he wants to say, in any way that pleases him. But the same expressions or the same thoughts coming from a person without 'soul' might well be strongly resented. 'Soul' gives a word an extra dimension, which completes its meaning and which, in many cases, can make an otherwise dangerous term completely inoffensive. 'Nigger' is a case in point. Used by a white person either to or about a black, it would be considered intolerably insulting by blacks, a reminder of the bad old days of slavery and oppression. But, in the mouth of a black person, it automatically becomes a 'soul' word. According to the occasion, it can show either hostility or fondness. A drunken husband can be a 'bad nigger', and a well-behaved child a 'good nigger'. But only if a black woman says so.

Black language, in the true sense of the terms, is therefore soul language. It makes up what might be called the black lexicon, words which black people feel to be peculiarly their own and function as racial identity labels. If and when a soul term becomes popular with whites, the people to whom it belonged will usually give up using it, partly because it has, so to speak, become polluted and partly because it has lost its secret nature. This has happened, for example, with 'strung-out' and 'uptight'.

Those whites, including a high proportion of our young people, who are emotionally committed to thinking of themselves as sharing the same interests and pursuing the same goals as the blacks, find it difficult even to allow the possibility that their black brothers and sisters have access to a language which they themselves will never be able to understand properly.

This predicament has been honestly and sensibly discussed in America, but so far very little in Britain. 'One of the main applications of black language', we have been reminded, 'has been to strengthen the in-group solidarity of black Americans to the specific exclusion of whites, and to deceive, confuse and conceal information from white people in general. Hence it is that an in-group black expression will often be dropped from black speech – or changed in meaning – as soon as it becomes widely known among non blacks. The use of such outmoded speech is aptly described by the black American phrase "talking dead", so that the first appearance in print of an originally black expression may not necessarily mark the time of its birth, but in a very real sense the time of its "death", perhaps after a long life in unrecorded black speech.'[4]

This, of course, is precisely the type of social phenomenon which is so difficult to reflect in the ordinary kind of dictionary, almost wholly dependent as it is on the fossilisation of words in print before they can be officially recognised or indeed before the fact of their existence is known at all to those who collect information for dictionaries.

But the ignorance of dictionary-makers, as inevitable as it is misleading, can be of another kind, where the speech of the black communities is concerned. There are many words which a dictionary of British English will categorise as imports from America, and which dictionaries of American English consider as American as hickory, baseball and apple pie, but which in fact come directly from West African languages, via the blacks of North America. The work that has been done on this is comparatively recent and it is of major importance, because it changes the pedigree of key American expressions and in this way increases the cultural dependence of the whites on the blacks, a development which is not likely to be welcome in every quarter. Somewhat ironically, the most original work in this field of research has been carried out by someone who is neither American nor black, David Dalby, of the School of Oriental and African Studies at the University of London.[5]

One of the reasons why the West African origins of these words had not been previously suspected is that their forms and pronunciations, but not their meanings, have coalesced with those existing white words. Illustrations of this are:

bug	in the sense of 'enthusiast' — nearly always in compounds – train-bug, golf-bug
bug	to annoy
bug	insect
cat	man, fellow, alone and in compounds
chick	girl, young woman
dig	understand, appreciate, pay attention to
dirt	earth, soil
guy	fellow, person
hep, hip	well-informed, alert, aware of what is going on
jazz	speed up, excite, act in an unrestrained way
jitter	tremble, shake
okay	all right
zombie	ghost

This is merely a selection from a long list. The lively, adaptive, democratic American language, second to none in vigour and appetite for change, now turns out to owe much of its expressiveness to people who were brought to the country in chains. These same people, previously thought to have been merely comic manglers and distorters of a vital part of the American birthright, the language of the Pilgrim Fathers, Benjamin Franklin and George Washington, are now revealed as a great creative influence on the American vocabulary, worthy to be ranked with their former masters.

It is not only the American language and American blacks that we are talking about. There has been a community of culture, not complete, it is true, but sufficiently far-reaching to make the phrase reasonably exact, between the blacks of the United States and the blacks of the West Indies and the Caribbean, and the main primary carriers of this common culture to Britain have been blacks belonging to the second group. There have, of course, been secondary carriers in abundance, mainly in the form of records, television programmes and films, but with these we are not at the moment concerned.

Black people, no matter where they live or come from, are popularly supposd to be noisy people, much given to loud music, loud singing and loud talking, especially in the streets. There is no doubt a good deal of truth in this, although it is worth pointing out that a great many British teenagers are not exactly quiet in their behaviour and that in few places is the noise level higher than in a disco in a British city. But the complaints about the noisy habits of our black fellow-citizens have mostly come from the whites over 40, not those under 20. The number of decibels generated by the West Indian community has been one of the great attractions for many British teenagers, who may well have found in black noise a source of great encouragement for their own white noise.

It can encourage and stimulate even those who make no secret about their dislike of blacks in Britain. As Colin MacInnes observed with typical shrewdness at the beginning of the 1970s, skinheads may hate blacks, but they love Reggae. 'It may be the rage, the exuberance, the manifest "hands off" tone of Reggae sound – and usual performance – together with the music's violently hypnotic beat that attracts rebellious white audiences.'[6]

Skinheads, however, are celebrated for their small vocabulary and for their preference for action to speech. They can hardly be described as great talkers and in this respect they are the complete antithesis to the black youths of urban America, whose delight in verbal play is one of their most attractive features. It is this, almost as much as their skin colour, which splits them off from their white contemporaries. The whites tend to understate, the blacks to overstate. The tense, almost monosyllabic prose of Hemingway and his imitators had nothing to offer black Americans. As the distinguished black writer, Ralph Ellison, said when explaining why his prose had to be entirely different from Hemingway's: 'I found that, when compared with the rich babble of idiomatic expression around me, a language full of imagery and gesture and rhetorical canniness, it was embarrassingly austere.'[7]

'Austere', in this context, could almost have been a synonym for 'dull, uninspiring', which is what many, perhaps most, blacks consider the speech and writing of white people to be. The same contrast exists between the religious services which appeal to black and white people. To whites, the black service and the black preaching appear exaggerated, wild and flamboyant, whereas to blacks the white service is flat and pointless. The culture of the American negro, under slavery, was inevitably oral and this tradition has been maintained into our own times. It is emphasised in the black devotion to 'rapping', a word which has little real meaning for white people, although they may understand intellectually what it means. 'Rapping' is impressive speech, or perhaps one should say speech designed to impress. It involves asserting one's own skill with words, building oneself up by one's talk, going one better than the other person, duelling with words. It is roughly comparable to the white habit of wise-cracking, in that both are a way of showing off. But wise-cracking is essentially epigrammatic and scores best by a pithy, economical use of words; 'rapping', on the other hand, is cumulative in its effect, the long rally as against the service ace. It is exemplified in its most extreme form by the street game known as 'playing the dozens', where the aim is, after a long and exciting battle of wits, to totally destroy someone else with words.

The blacks who came to Britain after the Second World War were familiar with 'rapping'; it was part of their style and culture, but they never practised it quite as skilfully and wholeheartedly as the blacks of the American cities. British teenagers in Bristol,

Southall or Notting Hill have only very rarely been able to hear 'rapping' of the vintage quality which one finds in Harlem. The word 'rap' itself has been fairly well known in Britain since the late 1960s, but in its journey across the Atlantic it has lost the flavour it had within the American black community and is used almost as a synonym for 'talk, chat', although usually with a suggestion of enthusiasm – so, 'I and the people I rap will think it is important',[8] 'goodly people to rap to'[9] and 'rapping with the band'.[10] It is also found as a noun – 'in the second part of his fascinating rap with me'[11] – but, here too, it has become, from the point of view of the black communities, a dead word. The whites have taken it over and the magic has departed. It has become a word like any other word.

But it is very doubtful if English teenagers have ever given much thought to the blackness or whiteness of a word. What is much more important is its feeling of modernity, its associations with the right kind of people. In any case, the black/white distinction, so far as Britain is concerned, has become strangely unreal during the past ten or fifteen years, as a generation of British-born black teenagers has grown up. They speak with the accent of their school and their district and, over the telephone, it is impossible to know if most of them are black or white. Britain is now full of black 18-year-olds with Cockney, Liverpool and Glasgow accents. It is not, however, only a matter of accent. The *whole* speech of many of these youngsters is entirely white – their vocabulary, the way they put their sentences together, their intonation. They are, if one is permitted to put it this way, black whites, just as there are now tens of thousands of brown whites, Indians and Pakistanis born in Britain, who sound as British as if their families had been here for generations.

Yet, side by side with the black whites are a considerable number of blacks of the same age who take great pride not only in being different, but in sounding different. These are the black blacks, the people who resist all temptations to become absorbed into British life. Most of them are to be found in areas where many black people are living together, the so-called black ghettoes, and where the proportion of black pupils in the local school is so high, often a majority, that the general tone and culture of the school is black, not white, and where the motivation to behave and sound like one's white fellow-pupils does not exist. It is interesting and significant to note that the phenomenon of remaining brown brown is rare among Indian and Pakistani boys and girls. Aggressively Indian Indians, deliberately exaggerating their cultural differences in public, are not easy to find, a fact which is often taken to indicate, with good reason, that Asians make more satisfactory immigrants than blacks, and not only in Britain. In saying this, one is not making a racist statement at all. Throughout history, it has been normal for immigrants to try to become indistinguishable members of the host community with all possible speed. For the original immigrants, this can rarely be completely achieved, although some make remarkably good attempts, but their children usually fade into the new background without much difficulty. The blacks, for understandable reasons, have proved the exception. Whether they like it or not, they have to be discussed as a separate case, for the very good reason that they have chosen to think of themselves as permanently separate and different, with a destiny that they cannot share with their white fellow-citizens.

And, at this point, we return to the sentence from Hebdige with which we began this chapter – 'The black man, by his presence, made everything possible' – and put an important question: 'Which black man?' Hebdige's epigram, like all epigrams, is too simple, stimulating as it may be. We are now, in the 1980s, in a position to sort out our black men and to distinguish four broad groups, each of which has had some degree of influence on the British people and their way of life, especially on those in the process of growing up.

The first category we might call the Exotic Black Man. This is the black man who reaches us only in images, the black man of films, stories, television programmes and recordings. He has been with us in one form or another for a very long time, certainly since the eighteenth century. For most of this period he has been a semi-comic figure, simple-minded, speaking a form of pidgin English, with a dog-like devotion to his white masters at his best, rebellious and treacherous at his worst, and always with a limited capacity for learning. First the American Civil War and then the break-up of Europe's African empires shattered the convenient old image of the faithful dog, but it remains unerased and unerasable in the background for a great many older people, although they have discovered the wisdom of keeping their outdated and, from the point of view of the young, dangerous attitudes to themselves. Now and again, however, yesterday's thinking emerges from hiding and proves remarkably popular with a public that has no business to exist. One thinks of Alf Garnett's outrageous statements about black people in the television comedies *Till Death Us Do Part* of ten and fifteen years ago and, more recently, the fictional Denis Thatcher's comments on wogs and coons in *Private Eye*'s 'Dear Bill' series. The fact that Alf Garnett was speaking with the voice of the working class and 'Dear Bill' with that of the upper middle class should not be overlooked. The stereotype of the funny black man, with very little between the ears, is one which established itself firmly among all classes in Britain, and it was strengthened, rather than weakened, one should note, by the fact that many British people, of both sexes, spent long periods in African countries as members of the civilian and military ruling class.

During the 1920s and 1930s the black man was permitted and even encouraged to make a career, often a highly lucrative career, for himself in the entertainment world, playing, singing, acting, boxing and wrestling. He could do this without asking to be taken seriously. It was a new and acceptable version of the comic, childlike black man. Paul Robeson, who was certainly not a comic figure, did not seriously interfere with the traditional image, because the songs he sang mostly echoed the old plantation days and his white audiences found that agreeably nostalgic.

But, in whatever form the Exotic Black Man reached Britain, the essential thing about him was that he did not live here. He was nearly always an American black, who represented one aspect of the culture of the United States. In no way was he a threat to British traditions and the British social system but, purely figuratively and without the slightest wish to be offensive, one could say that he manured the ground for the great crop of black culture which was to be planted in Britain during the 1940s and 1950s. He was a popular entertainer and, as such, he was identified with pleasure and leisure, not with earning a living. He had a deep-throated idiom, which was summed up in the words of 'Ole Man River' and 'The Camptown Races'; he was always smiling and he was easily caricatured.

Our second type of black man was fundamentally different. He came from the Caribbean and the West Indies and one could see and hear him in the flesh. Moreover, he had a British passport and he was here to stay, to settle and to breed, not on a passing visit. He was in the labour market and the housing market and, as such, he was in direct competition with the white population, or at least with the working-class section of it, since our post-1945 black immigrants included extremely few people with a middle-class or professional background. They were allowed into the country in the first place because there was a serious shortage of people to do menial work and the first generation of them counted themselves lucky to find such jobs, at rates of pay far in excess of what they would have received at home, if, indeed, they had been able to discover any work at all. On the whole, they seem to have been grateful for the ópportunity to start what they expected would be a better and more prosperous life. Many, but inevitably not all, of them worked hard and saved enough to be able to buy a house, and quite a number studied, acquired paper qualifications and moved into white-collar jobs. Hospitals in the bigger towns began to train and employ black nurses.

Paradoxically, it was the ability and anxiety of the more enterprising blacks to buy houses which created what we can now see to have been the most serious problem, the development of areas within the larger cities which became largely or mainly inhabited by black people. Blacks with money bought houses which were inhabited by blacks without money, and as more and more blacks moved into places like Brixton, Notting Hill and the St Pauls district of Bristol, more and more whites moved out, creating a situation in which the second generation of Britain's black population often had fewer direct contacts with white people than their parents had had.

Mixed up with them, not always easily, were the third type of black, direct from Africa, especially Nigeria and Ghana. Most of these came from relatively well-to-do families, with the money to send their sons to England to study. The intermingling of these two kinds of black people provided Colin MacInnes, the first to take the trouble to investigate the life of Britain's new black population with the care and sympathy it deserved, with the raw material for his novels. The encounters between the educated Africans and the uneducated and, alas, often criminal West Indians gave MacInnes the opportunity to depict both cultures in a wonderfully illuminating way.

Mr Karl Marx Bo, from Freetown, speaks in Palmerstonian, if not Johnsonian, English but with an accent which the text cannot reproduce.

'Here in London, I am studying law,' he told me.

'That means, I suppose, that you'll be going into politics?'

'Inevitably. We must make the most of our learning here in London. Emancipation, sir, is our ultimate objective. I predict that in the next ten years, or less, the whole of West Africa will be a completely emancipated federation.'

'Won't the Nigerians gobble you up? Or Dr. Nkrumah?'

'No, sir. Such politicians clearly understand that national differences of that nature are a pure creation of colonialism. Once we have federation, such regional distinctions will all fade rapidly away.'

'Well, jolly good luck to you.'

'Oh, yes! You say so! But like all Englishmen, I conceive you view with reluctance the prospect of our freedom?'

'Oh, but we give you the education to get it.'

'Not give, sir. I pay for my university courses through profits my family have made in the sale of cocoa.'[12]

But there are other MacInnes characters our fourth group of blacks – whose language is far from Johnsonian.

"I hose boys they sink I stupit – "Boos-a-man" (Bushman) they call me, becos I come out from my home in him interiors, not city folk like those wikit waterfronk boys . . . ' He ruminated, flashing his eyes about. 'They sink I stupit because of no educasons. But (crescendo) my blood better than their blood! My father sieftan (chieftain)!'

'Yes?'

'Yes. I sief's son.'[13]

Which blacks, one may well say, is one talking about? It would be a little absurd to claim that either of the two quoted above is likely to have had a great deal of direct influence on British speech during the past thirty years. But this, one imagines, is not the point that Hebdige was trying to make. It is not that white teenagers or, for that matter, white adults have imitated the habits of black people, but rather that the sudden appearance of many thousands of blacks in the community has unsettled the British, of all ages, who were already here. Questioning everything and accepting very little, our black immigrants, and even more their children, have encouraged white boys and girls to look at society and themselves in a new way. Previously they had to find a tolerable compromise between their own wishes and opinions and those of their parents. Now they had as well to accommodate themselves to an alien culture in their midst, a culture which contained many features which they found extremely attractive, but at the same time a culture which rejected them, because they were white.

The accommodation has not worked itself out in words. 'It is on the plane of aesthetics, in dress, dance, music, in the whole rhetoric of style, that we find the dialogue between black and white most subtly and comprehensively recorded, albeit in code. We can watch played out on the loaded surfaces of British working-class youth culture, a phantom history of race relations since the war.'[14] And that history is one of admiring and hating, envying and despising blacks, both at the same time. There is a certain parallel with the German attitude towards the Jews, which produced tensions and anxieties from which persecution and the concentration camps came to appear as the only escape.

CHAPTER SEVEN
Youth and the Law

Twenty years ago Terence Morris took a careful look at the extent to which British adolescents were involved with the police and the courts, and at the offences with which they were charged. He made no specific distinction between white boys and girls and black ones, but one gathers from certain clues in his published work that his main concern had been with the white community. His general conclusion was, assuming one accepts it, that 'there has been no growth in teenage delinquents, only a growth in the number of teenagers and in the number of cases brought before the courts'.[1] Teenagers, in other words, were no better or worse than they had always been, but society, for some reason, had come to consider it advisable that youthful misdeeds were better dealt with by the proper process of law, instead of by a cuff and a warning from the local policeman. Morris wrote:

> So much attention has been concentrated on juvenile delin-
> quency in particular and teenage misbehaviour in general that
> for what must be a sizeable proportion of the adult population
> the term teenager has become virtually synonymous with delin-
> quent, sexually promiscuous, antisocial youth. The postwar
> period is littered with cast-off pejorative epithets describing
> successive stages in the development of contemporary youth
> culture – spiv, coshboy, Teddy Boy, beatnik – each an
> imprecise, inaccurate or deliberately distorted term used in a
> wide variety of public contexts and often by those who ought to
> have known better.[2]

In a similar vein – 'there's nothing remarkable or different about today's teenagers, boys and girls are much the same as they always were' – Ray Gosling wrote about adolescent morals[3] and Michael

Schofield about their sexual behaviour.[4] The Eppels took a somewhat broader sweep and concerned themselves with teenage values, their method being to discover the kind of people teenagers used as models. The most glamorous occupation for boys, they established, was not 'gangster', 'pop musician' or even 'burglar', but 'sportsman', and for girls, 'star'. But there is in fact little evidence, they concluded, 'that these young working people, even at their most romantic, are seriously influenced by filmstars, pop heroes, or sports idols'.[5] Such figures were fantasy characters around whom dreams could be woven, a compensation for one's own much more pedestrian existence. A hundred or five hundred years earlier, the repertoire of heroes would necessarily have been different, for the good reason that there were no filmstars or successful and well-promoted footballers at that time, and no mass communications to create nationally-accessible personalities. The world outside one's own immediate district was, for most people, a very vague place and heroes had to be either local, William Jones, the blacksmith, or generic, a soldier, an explorer, a rich titled lady.

Yet, whatever the period, most teenagers and, for that matter, a great many adults, too, have a very unrealistic view of the world. Their idols are frequently quite unworthy to occupy such a role and their folk devils are in fact much more desirable characters than current myths allow them to be. One of the most disturbing processes that affects everyone in the course of his or her life is the discovery that few notabilities deserve the fame and prestige which society, or sections of society, has given them, that idols do indeed turn out to have had feet of clay. Generals, admirals, statesmen and dukes, to say nothing of bishops, kings and actresses, all have a way of being singularly unheroic once the myth surrounding them has withered away and the surface gloss has lost its shine. One can hardly bear to contemplate what the effect of a book with a title like *The Truth about Elvis Presley* will be, but it will surely come, and when it does the by-then ageing faithful will feel, at least for a while, that much of the light has gone from their world.

A large part of one's life is lived vicariously, in the imagination, and most of what goes on in one's mind is, fortunately, unknown to the outside world. The ability to protect one's inner life in this way is perhaps God's greatest gift to humanity. Without it, we should not be able to survive very long. Our personality is built of the interplay, the dialogue, between our private thoughts and emotions and the surface which we allow the world to see and assess. But the imagination has to be fed. Without stimuli from what passes as the real world, it could not exist. Equally, certain of our fantasies may eventually be transformed into actions, sometimes very dangerous actions indeed, sometimes of import-ance to no-one but ourselves. Our reading and our watching of films and television programmes can turn us into fantasy international footballers, ballerinas, round-the-world lone yachtsmen or simply members of the class of the rich and idle. But it can also produce, on occasion, all-too-real thieves, muggers, rapists, baby-snatchers, picture-slashers and murder-ers, people who have been impelled to act out roles which they first met in the form of fiction.

It is the failure to distinguish between the real and the fantasy, the passive and latent and the active, which has been responsible for so many of the misjudgements and misunderstandings con-cerning teenage habits. Because a person is aware of certain words, it does not follow that he uses them. Because he is sur-rounded by socially dangerous people, in his school or in the district where he lives, he himself may not necessarily be a social menace at all. The young, even more than adults, have a well-developed instinct for taking on protective colouring, and what they say and do cannot be taken as reliable evidence of what they understand or think.

With these general considerations in mind, let us construct a small glossary of words which belong to those fields of activity in which teenagers have shown themselves most likely to fall foul of the law, enquiring at the same time, asking ourselves at the same time, four questions:

1. Do I myself understand the meaning of this word?
2. Would I use it?
3. If it is not a word I would use, what would my reasons be?
4. What picture do I have of the kind of people who would use the word easily and naturally?

We will group these potentially explosive or disreputable words under the headings of sex, drugs, violence, and the law and its agents. All have been in current use during the past thirty years, and some we may wish to reject simply because they feel dated.

All have been identified to a greater or lesser degree with the Permissive Society, the Forces of Corruption, the Enemies of Law and Order, Decadence or whatever one's own favourite phrase may be to describe movements working to undermine the Establishment and overthrow the status quo.

SEX

Art   Soft porn, soft-focus nudes. Used straight, as a technical term by advertisers, but jokingly and ironically by everyone else.
   'Parisienne showgirl has private collection of revealing Art Photographs for sale.'[6]

Come across   To dispense sexual favours. A recent extension of an existing British expression, found soon after the First World War, which meant 'be pleasant or willing', with no specific sexual significance.
   'Despite an evening of boozing, she wouldn't come across.'[7]

Come out   Openly declare one's homosexuality. Used by and about both male and female homosexuals.
   'After being spotted on the march by some of his pupils, John came out at school.'[8]
   'The Alex Dobkin come out tour'.[9]

Cruise   To go out with the idea of picking up a sexual partner. Used mainly by male homosexuals.
   'Being active in a gay collective does not usually mean a renunciation of cruising the gay bars and discotheques.'[10]

Crumpet   Women and girls considered collectively and with an emphasis on their sexual attractions and willingness. A mainly, but not exclusively, male expression, used by all social classes and hardly ever heard outside Britain.
   'We're not heavily into crumpet on the road.'[11]

Cunt   The vagina, and hence, symbolically, a woman. This, the second most common and, until recent years, the most taboo of all sexual words, has been part of the British vocabulary since at least the fourteenth century and probably a good deal longer. In the early 1950s, the previously unthinkable happened: a strong, deliberate and partially successful attempt was made to break the taboo. The underground press, the readers of which were mostly below the age of 25, used the bluntest and crudest of sexual terms in order to shock or try to shock as many people as possible. This policy aimed at showing how sexually liberated the writers were. Whether the results were precisely what was intended is a matter of opinion, but the limits of the possible had certainly been extended and the power of certain words will probably never be quite as strong again.

One important consequence has been to establish a divide between the generations in the matter of sexual vocabulary, with younger people showing a good deal more forthrightness than their elders. This is even more marked in the case of women and girls, although the change should not be exaggerated and it should be noted that the social context of a remark still makes a good deal of difference to the degree of explicitness.

Dyke A lesbian, usually of markedly male appearance. This word has been current for about fifty years, although its use, until recently, has been very restricted. Since the 1950s, as part of the general enfranchisement of the sexual lexicon, it has become much more widely employed, usually in a derogatory sense. Even now, however, it is a term which few women would actually use, although they might well understand its meaning In lesbian circles, it is considered vaguely insulting.

'He made the mistake of calling her a dyke.'[12]

Resentment to it may just possibly be connected with the fact that from the mid-nineteenth century until the 1920s, 'dyke' or 'dike' was a distinctly low colloquial expression for 'lavatory'.

The adjective, 'dykey', is an equal favourite with the underground press and its readers.

'I am tired of dykey sales ladies.'[13]

Fuck Both as a verb and as a noun, this most common and explicit of all sexual words is at least two centuries old. What is new and indeed revolutionary is the extent to which the term has been allowed out of hiding during the past thirty years or so. It is now used without any noticeable hesitation or timidity by the kind of people, especially women and girls, who would at one time have been appalled at the thought of uttering it. Much of its former strength and forbidden magic has now departed from it, to the point at which it is almost a flat technical term, like 'walk' or 'eat'.

Like the underground press, feminist publications have made deliberate and frequent use of blunt sexual terms in order to shock conventional opinion and to emphasise their attitude of enlightened frankness in these matters. So we have, as a matter of course:

'Wendy, the "easy" girl, without quite realising it, gets fucked at a party.'[14]

The compounds of this all-purpose word are increasingly numerous and widely used, although most of them appear to pass out of fashion within a few years.

Kinky In the 1950s and early 1960s, 'kinky' implied sexual deviation, with a strong hint of sadism. A 'kinky' person was a deviant or pervert of some kind. Soon after this, however, the whole business of whips, high boots and leather clothing began to appear laughable, rather than sinister, to those people – the great majority – whose own tastes did not incline in that direction, and it is now close to being a joke word, among the young. As an exclamation, it is always spoken on rising tones and with a marked pause between the first and second syllable.

Knee-length leather boots, which became acceptable and respectable fashion wear in the mid-1960s, were originally and for obvious reasons known as 'kinky boots', but the tag disappeared within a year or two. The association with whip-wielding ladies remained clearly noticeable, however, in 'One might as well prosecute shops for selling kinky boots'.[15]

Lay The dictionary definition, 'to have sexual intercourse with', is both accurate and inadequate. It does not allow for the fact that, as a verb, this is a sexist word. Men lay women, but women do not lay men. The noun, 'lay', is more broadminded. It can indicate a person of either sex who is available for sexual activity, but refers more usually to a female.

The word, in this sense, arrived in Britain during the Second World War and therefore before the Teenage Revolution exploded here. It is widely understood, but has never enjoyed the same popularity or classlessness here as in the country of its birth. The British working class, of all ages, has never really taken to it.

Lech A lecher, a womaniser. This essentially teenage and pop-culture abbreviation became common during the late 1960s, but is heard much less nowadays. It was always used more frequently by girls than by boys and, in general, by those with an above-average education. A 'lech', unlike a 'lecher', could be of any age, and young ones were as abundant as old ones.

Les A lesbian. The usual abbreviation in Britain, especially among the young, although on the upper levels of society 'lezzie' is also found. 'Lesbian' is not included in the original six-volume *Oxford English Dictionary*, although it is dealt with in the later *Supplement*. The word, in its full form, appears to have entered the language as an educated colloquialism and did not become part of Standard English until the 1930s, which was still an age of innocence, when very few people knew of the existence of homosexuals of either sex.

Queen A male homosexual, generally of the more obvious, flamboyant, or outrageous kind. With the spelling 'quean', the word had existed since the eighteenth century, possibly longer, but in Britain it had become virtually obsolete by the 1930s. In Australia, however, it lingered on. In the 1950s it came back into common use, although this time always spelt 'queen'. There is no great mystery about its revival. The new public tolerance of homesexuality and the prurient journalistic interest in it created the need for a vocabulary with which to discuss previously avoided subjects.

Queer As a noun, it is 'a male homosexual' and as an adjective, 'possessing homosexual characteristics'. A word nowadays known to almost everyone of whatever social class and able to be used in drawing-room company. It is, one should note, never used by homosexuals themselves.

Randy Sexually aroused, excited. Until the 1950s, this late-eighteenth-century word nearly always referred to men. It is a significant mark of postwar change that it is now used indifferently by and about both women and men. As the songwriters make clear, women are now acknowledged to have desires, and to be randy is the privilege of both sexes. But this mainly British expression causes certain problems in America, where the Christian name Randy is common.

Screw   Amongst its several different meanings – 'a prison officer', 'to exploit', 'to look up and down' – 'screw' continues to mean 'to have sexual intercourse', as it has done since the eighteenth century. In recent years, however, there has been an important change of usage. Before the 1950s it was, with rare exceptions, restricted to the male vocabulary and usually as a transitive verb. It is now, with much of its taboo departed, widely used by the young, especially working-class, of both sexes, and it can be either a transitive or intranstive verb.

'Loving (non-screwing) relationship.'[16]

Shag   This eighteenth-century word for 'to have intercourse' has remained in common use until the present day, but with one important change during the past thirty years. Until *c.* 1950 a man could 'shag' a woman, but a woman could neither 'shag' a man nor 'shag', although she might, as part of her traditionally passive role in society, 'be shagged'. The postwar campaign for women's rights has improved the situation somewhat.

'Woodbine Lizzy. Shags like a rattlesnake, doesn't she?'[17] would not have been possible a decade earlier.

Straight   This is one of the key underground, alternative words. It sums up everything the anti-Establishment groups felt themselves to be fighting against. So, from the 1960s onwards, it has come to be almost a synonym for 'conventional', with, in appropriate contexts, the specialised meaning of 'heterosexual'. Used in this sense, 'straight' emerged considerably later than its opposite, 'bent'.

So, 'the man I've met has a largely straight circle of friends'[18] and 'if he satisfies a straight woman'.[19]

Tart   This word is used by the young in two distinct senses, a fact which is liable to cause outside observers some confusion. Its most usual meaning is 'a girl interested in and prepared for sexual activity, but not a prostitute'. To members of an older generation, on the other hand, 'tart' almost always did mean 'prostitute'. There is, however, a secondary meaning, 'a flashy, pretentious person of either sex'. The context will usually, but not always, indicate which meaning is intended.

Turn on   A difficult phrase to interpret, because it may or may not have sexual connotations. 'Here's one blowing gently in your ear trying to turn you on'[20] is certainly sexual, but 'Everybody is very turned on by *IT*'[21] conveys a less specific kind of excitement or stimulation, although it is true that, in the case of teenagers attending a pop concert, one can never be sure where sexual excitement begins and ends. A further complication is the use of 'turned on' to mean 'aware of the real circumstances'.

Wank   Until the mid-1960s, the only meaning was 'masturbate'. From then on, one finds the figurative sense of 'indulge oneself, go on and on about a particular topic' increasingly used. This is now very common among the young and fashionable with older trendies. So, too, is 'wanker', meaning 'an incompetent, dull person, someone incapable of originality or creativity'. Football crowds are particularly fond of this word and it is used a good deal in the pop-music world.

'They're just a bunch of wankers, who see us as a way of making money'.[22]

But the old meaning continues with 'wank mag' – that is, 'a pornographic magazine'. This phrase is undoubtedly an echo of 'Yank mag', and is now well past its peak of popularity.

Whack off   To masturbate. A term current among teenagers of both sexes. Its origins appear to be entirely post-Second World War, and there is something of a public-school flavour about it.

'Her mother catches Janis in the bath, singing the Kozmic Blues and whacking off.'[23]

The popularity of this expression among teenagers makes it difficult for them to use the word 'whacked' for 'exhausted'. 'Whacked' is therefore largely confined nowadays to older, especially middle-class, people who are unfamiliar with 'whack off'.

What has clearly happened to the British sexual vocabulary during the past thirty years or so is that it has gradually demystified itself and consequently is much weaker in its overtones and effects. For each successive generation of teenagers during this period, the kind of words which their parents and grandparents would never have dreamed of uttering in public or, for the most part, in private either, have become 'ordinary' terms of expression, with no particularly remarkable force to them. This is a change which most older people find difficult to understand. The most effective way of explaining the situation to them is to suggest that their children and grandchildren use words previously considered taboo much as a foreigner would – that is, without attaching any instinctive potency to them and without any fear of lifted eyebrows. Sex is no longer a behind-closed-doors subject. Whether this means that it has been downgraded or upgraded is a matter of opinion. One should, however, point out that what one called, rather pompously, the agencies of social control – parents, teachers, the police, the courts – are apt to come to wrong conclusions where the language of teenagers is concerned. If they know about, say, sex or drugs and if they talk about these things in a matter-of-fact way, it may or may not prove that they transfer talk into action. If someone is not horrified by a word, it cannot be assumed that the same person would not hold back from the action represented by the word.

A good example of this is the vocabulary of homosexuality, with which young people today have a much greater degree of familiarity than their parents have, partly, no doubt, because they are accustomed to see these words printed in the kind of magazines they read. But only a very small proportion of them are homosexuals or lesbians and there is a strong probability that many of them are far from clear as to exactly what homosexuals and lesbians get up to. They are, however, much more likely to be well informed in these matters than their parents are, because the spirit of the age encourages, rather than inhibits, discussion of them. For this reason, the present book would have been difficult to research, write and publish in the 1950s. In the 1930s such a project would have been impossible and, in any case, it would have been irrelevant to the conditions of the time. The Teenage Revolution and everything it implies had not occured.

DRUGS

The point can be further illustrated by means of a selection from the very long list of expressions associatied with the practice of drug-taking, expressions which simply did not exist before the

1940s and with which everyone under the age of 45 has, consciously or not, grown up. It is interesting to note that there has been no corresponding new vocabulary in respect of drinking. In Britain, unlike Saudi Arabia, the buying and selling of alcohol is perfectly legal and, largely for this reason, there has been no strong incentive to invent a special vocabulary which will link the law-breakers together and raise their morale. Drinking has not been either a fashionable or a dare-devil pastime among the young in the way that drugs, sex and, to a lesser extent, violence have and so it has not produced an impressive spawning of new expressions.

The very small selection of drug words which follows is intended both to illustrate the extent to which a minority habit has influenced the language and also to give those who missed the drug age an opportunity to check on their knowledge or ignorance. Once again, it seems wise to point out that most adolescents have a highly developed imitative streak in them. They like to conform to the fashion and to what their immediate social group is doing, wearing and saying. It comforts them to appear knowledgeable and sophisticated about matters on which they have no personal experience or inclination at all. Being superficially conformist is an art which most people learn young. What is new about the situation produced by and reflected in the Teenage Revolution is that adolescents have been playing the game of conformity outwardly to their own culture, rather than, as before, to that of the adult world.

And with that we pass on to our mini-glossary of drug-taking.

Acid Lysergic acid. The most common term for the drug. Outsiders are more likely to call it LSD.

Bad trip Bad, confusing or frightening experience resulting from taking LSD. Also used for any kind of unpleasant experience, not necessarily as a result of taking drugs.

Blocked High on drugs.

Blow, have a Smoke marijuana. An interesting extension of meaning: 'blow' was used in the sense of an ordinary tobacco-filled cigarette in the 1920s.

Bombhead Someone who takes large quantities of stimulant drugs.

Brought down Depressed. Originally used in drug circles to describe the aftermath of a drug experience, and then, more generally, in the pop-music world.

'That tour was blown out and we were very brought down.'[24]

Carry Possess illegal drugs.

Charge Take marijuana.

Coke Cocaine.

Come down (1) To emerge from a drug stupour. (2) Depressing period, when the effects of a drug are wearing off.

Consciousness Awareness. A key word for hippies, linked to drug experiences.

Deal To sell drugs.

Dope Drugs. In the 1950s it meant 'hard drugs', but later it came to mean specifically marijuana and hashish.

Drop To take drugs orally, especially LSD.

Druggie Person who takes drugs.

Gear Drugs.

Grass Marijuana.

Habit Drug dependency.

Hash Hashish. A word used by devotees to distinguish the resin product from 'grass', and by casual users and outsiders as a general term for the drug.

Head (1) Someone who takes drugs, usually marijuana. Used only by drug-takers and their associates, it can have a wider meaning, 'someone who subscribes to the attitudes of the underground'. (2) Mind, thoughts, state of mind. A word much favoured by drug-takers, who are particularly interested in changes of consciousness.

High Under the influence of drugs or some other stimulant. Usually suggests a pleasant experience.

Hit Swig of alcohol, inhalation of marijuana cigarette, occasionally shot of other drug.

Hold To carry drugs.

Horse Heroin.

Hump Period of the peak of a drug experience.

Jack up To inject a drug.

Jay A cigarette containing marijuana. From the initial letter of 'joint' (q.v.).

Joint Home-made cigarette containing marijuana. The most common British expression and the one most widely understood by those outside drug circles.

Junk Any narcotic drug, most often heroin.

Line Dose of cocaine, so called because when inhaled it is arranged in a narrow line beforehand.

Loaded High on drugs.

Narc Policeman engaged on narcotic offences. Used by members of the drug culture, and not to be confused with the old-established 'nark', a police informer.

Pilled up Under the influence of amphetamines.

Pot Marijuana, cannabis. The most respectable word and the most widely understood. Except as a joke, 'pot' quickly became used only by people who did not themselves take the drug.

Psychodelia   The culture surrounding mind-expanding drugs.

Psychodelic   (1) Associated with or the result of drug-use in general. (2) Anything linked to the use of LSD.

Push   To sell illegal drugs. Until the late 1960s, the word was used mainly by those concerned personally with drugs and the drug trade, but now it is in general use.

Red   Barbiturate.

Reefer   Marijuana cigarette. After the early 1960s, this was rarely used by people who indulged in the drug, but it continued to form part of the vocabulary of journalists.
    '. . . prosecuted for selling reefers to unsuspecting teenagers.'[25]

Ripped   High on drugs or drink.

Roach   End of a marijuana cigarette.

Rush   Adrenalin flow as a stimulant drug begins to have an effect.

Score   (1) Buy or acquire drugs. 'Everybody scores hash here.'[26] (2) Person who sells drugs. 'Your next score doesn't like your face.'[27]

Shoot up   Inject a drug.

Skin   Paper used for rolling marijuana cigarettes.

Smoke   To smoke marijuana.

Speed   Amphetamines. An addict's term.

Spiked   Drugged unknowingly, laced (of a drink). Originally part of the drug-taker's specialised vocabulary, it has since achieved much wider currency.
    'Almost immediately I was spiked with wine and acid.'[28]

Splif   Cigarette containing marijuana. In the 1950s, in general use among drug-takers. Now mostly confined to West Indians.

Steamed   High on drugs.

Stoned   High on drugs. Used in the older sense of 'drunk' only by people who are unaware of its association with drugs.
   '5000 stoned, tripping, mad, friendly, festive, hippies.'[29]

Stoned out   High on drugs.

Straight   Not under the influence of drugs.

Strung out   Addicted to drugs, behaving with the obsessiveness of an adict.

Tab   Tablet, pill. Used, only by addicts, to describe a dose of LSD, not of other drugs which come in tablet form.

Toke   (1) To inhale from a marijuana cigarette. (2) An inhalation from a marijuana cigarette.

Trip   (1) Experience caused by drugs, usually LSD or mescalin. (2) To take LSD.

Tripped out   Under the influence of LSD, having the senses disturbed.

Turn on   To smoke marijuana. Originally a hippy expression.

Use   To use a drug regularly. 'Some are still using and unhappy.'[30]

Weed   Marijuana. Originally it meant 'tobacco'. In the sense of 'marijuana' it had its heyday in the 1950s. By the mid-1960s it was dead, except as a joke.

VIOLENCE

There is a whole new vocabulary of violence, reflecting the growth of teenage gangs and of what one might call aggression culture during the 1950s and 1960s. Among the most widely used expressions within this field have been the following.

Aggravation   (1) Violence, unpleasantness. A London word, taken up more widely in the 1970s. (2) Hostile treatment, especially from the police.

Aggro merchant   Aggressive person, fighter.

Boot, in **Put the boot in**   To use violence, fight.

Bootboy   Member of aggressive, usually skinhead, street gang.

Bundle   (1) A fight. (2) To fight.
   Originally working-class word, but with the increased prestige of violence, it has gone up in the world in recent decades.

Punch-up   Fight, brawl. Originally associated with the working-class end of the youth-culture spectrum.

Run-in   Battle, fight.

Steam in   To move in to get involved in a fight.

All of these are teenage euphemisms for what are often very unpleasant incidents indeed, involving the use of such unsophisticated weapons as chains, iron bars, studded belts and vicious kinds of knuckle-dusters. Severe injuries, involving hospital treatment, often result and are expected as a normal feature of the game. The use of such comparatively gentle expressions as 'bundle' and 'steam in' to describe such activities is interesting. By toning down the violence in this way, it is made to appear almost as a normal and unremarkable part of daily life, calling for no particular attention on the part of society or the law.

THE LAW AND ITS AGENTS

For the fighting, drug-taking, mugging, thieving elements among teenagers, the police and the whole machine of justice and punishment not unnaturally represents the enemy and a new vocabulary has been created to emphasise this and to reinforce solidarity among the real and potential law-breakers. Boys and girls who are never in trouble with the police use the same words, or some of them, as a matter of fashion and conformity. So the police are 'pigs', 'blue meanies', 'bill' and 'the fuzz'; someone who is discovered in possession of drugs is 'bust', and someone against whom no evidence can be found is 'clean'. To co-operate with the police or to show any sympathy with their social function is to be guilty of treason to one's age-group.

But one has to reckon even so with the apparent paradox that a surprisingly high proportion of teenagers would not dream of uttering many of the words which are popularly supposed to be their words, words which exist to bind them together as a soical force to be reckoned with. Not infrequently, they have only the vaguest idea of what the words mean. The teenagers' trade union turns out to have been a rather shaky affair after all.

If one assembles a list of fifty or so of the expressions which one knows to have been in current use among teenagers during the past thirty years or so and presents them to what seems to be a reasonably representative selection of 16–21-year-olds, the result can be very surprising. One asks, first, 'Do you know what this expression means?', then, 'Would you yourself use it?', and lastly, 'If you wouldn't use it, why wouldn't you?', and the experience suggests that the answer to the third question is likely to take four forms.

1. *I would have used it once, but I've outgrown it.*
   'Childish'; 'Not now'; 'Little girl'; 'Doesn't suit someone of my age.'
2. *This isn't my style at all.*
   'It's not me'; 'Not in my vocabulary'; 'Wouldn't come into my life'; 'Doesn't come naturally to me'; 'Not my group'; 'Public school'.
3. *The expression is out of date. I should seem ridiculous if I were to use it nowadays.*
   'Quaint'; 'Sixties'; 'Obsolete'; 'My mother says it'; 'Belongs to the immediate past'.
4. *I don't like it. I find it unpleasant.*

'Derogatory to the police'; 'Inelegant'; 'Too slangy'; 'Sexploita-
tion'; 'Sounds awful'; 'Patronising'; 'Makes me cringe with
embarrassment'.

Most people, of any age, are anxious to appear all of a piece.
Having decided, at least temporarily, what their place and role in
society are, they do their best to make sure that the way they look,
sound and behave all contribute to the desired total effect. One
must not wear clothes, have one's hair done, eat, drink or talk in a
style appropriate to the wrong age or cultural group. It is as
embarrassing to use yesterday's words as yesterday's fashions,
except, as we have pointed out earlier, ironically. Vocabulary in
itself is not, however, the most important feature of one's speech.
How one says a word is as socially critical as the word itself.
Language labels, the speech badges which distinguish one person
and one group from another, are of three kinds. There are, first,
the words which mark one off as belonging to a particular cultural group, the words which link each member of that group to the
others. Second, there are the ways of saying not only the special
words, but the whole of the language one uses – the accent, the
tune, the pauses, the projections, the playing-downs, the half-
smile, the spit in the voice. And, third, there are the words one
takes care not to use, the pronunciations and stresses one avoids,
the intonations which put one in the wrong social box. The first
two of these one might call the positive labels, the third the
negative label.

Labels of all three kinds will, of course, come and go, and one
of the greatest difficulties which one generation experiences in
trying to communicate with another is the failure to realise that
different concepts and attitudes of mind have become taboo or
obscene and that yesterday's impossibilities are now possible. At
one time, a song called 'The Chocolate-Coloured Coon' was
entirely permissible. Now, the use of the word 'coon' is sufficient
to put one in the Denis Thatcher group. Equally, the older
generation today finds the attitude of many, if not most, of the
young towards drugs, sex, violence and music largely incomprehensible. To be unfamiliar with the finer shades of meaning of
the vocabulary which describes these phenomena in their modern
form is to confess to being a member of another tribe. Yet it
would be foolish to pretend that everyone under 25 takes drugs,
engages in street warfare, sleeps with the first comer and revels in

discos and loud pop music. Such a blanket categorisation is simply not true and, as my own researches have shown quite clearly, there are a great many so-called 'youth words' which a substantial part of today's 'youth' do not know.

Outsiders – that is, older people – often find it very difficult to read the fine print of youth culture and to recognise the subtle distinctions and sub-divisions which exist within it. One's judgement is confused by superficial similarities, like jeans, Coke, beards and long loose hair. But it is precisely because the uniform is so universal, because the person unfamiliar with sheep cannot tell one sheep from another, that the individual underneath the uniform has to be sought with greater care. This is especially true of what one might call uniform words. If one has only written evidence at one's disposal, the very significant variation of tone and pattern between one social group and another is missed. It is for these reasons that our notions of the speech of the past are so unsatisfactory and no doubt misleading. The written word tells such a tiny part of the story, and our ancestors would certainly find many of our reconstructions and assumptions ludicrously wrong.

What one loses particularly is the subtle, but enormously important, symbolism of doing or saying something 99 per cent as the convention dictates, the remaining 1 per cent being one's own personal contribution, the twist, possibly unnoticed by most of one's contemporaries, which allows one to remain fully human and an individual.

Notes and References

CHAPTER 1: WHAT REVOLUTION?

1. Throughout this book 'revolution' is used in general sense of 'fundamental and far-reaching change'. Political revolution, involving the overthrow of an existing system of government, is not necessarily implied.
2. Peter Laslett, in *Listener*, 11 January 1962, p. 53. This was the third of three talks, all reprinted in the *Listener*, given under the general title of 'The Social Revolution of Our Time'.
3. This was even more true of the United States, where four million boys and girls became 18 in 1965, compared with two million in 1956. Even so, as was pointed out by an American observer in Erik H. Erikson (ed.), *Youth: Change and Challenge* (New York: Basic Books, 1961) p. 133: 'At the time of the signing of the Declaration of Independence, half the nation was under eighteen. We do not touch this proportion today.'
4. James S. Coleman, *The Adolescent Society* (New York: The Free Press, 1961) p. 3.
5. Peter Wilmott, *Adolescent Boys of East London* (London: Routledge, 1966) p. 36.
6. Expressions such as 'his or her', 'he or she' will not always be used in this book when both sexes are implied. For ease of reading the simpler 'his' or 'he' will be used.
7. Graham Turner, 'Ladies will be Ladies', *Sunday Telegraph*, 12 July 1981. Turner makes a very similar point in his previous article about Eton, 5 July 1981. The majority of Eton boys, he says, prefer to conceal the fact when they are with strangers. They 'reach for their camouflage'. But, he points out, 'accents can give the game away'. The boys reckon that only 10 per cent now have *real* Etonian accents and almost everyone seems both delighted and relieved. 'It's only grandmothers who have really awful Etonian voices', said Tony Ray, the Senior Housemaster, while Tom, who took his A levels this half (i.e. term) admits candidly that 'you keep your accent down because of other people'.
8. Angela Rippon, well known as a BBC television newsreader during the 1970s.
9. Alan S. C. Ross, in *Neuphilologische Mitteilungen*, LX, 21 (1954).
10. Alan S. C. Ross, with Robin Brackenbury, 'U and Non-U Today', *New Society*, 22 August 1968.
11. His own analysis of his life is to be found in his autobiography, Ray Gosling, *Sum Total* (London: Faber, 1962).

12. Ibid., p. 53.
13. Brian Morris, *An Introduction to Mary Quant's London* (London Museum, 1973) p. 7.
14. Dennis Chapman, 'The Autonomous Generation', *Listener*, 17 January 1963.
15. Alan Little, 'The Young Affluents', *Listener*, 9 May 1963.
16. Bernard Davies, 'Non-Swinging Youth', *New Society*, 3 July 1969.

CHAPTER 2: ATTITUDES TO WORDS

1. Basil Bernstein (ed.), *Class, Codes and Control*, vol. 1: *Theoretical Studies Towards a Sociology of Language* (London: Routledge & Kegan Paul, 1971)
2. Ibid, p. 28.
3. Ibid, p. 28.
4. Ibid, p. 28.
5. Ibid, p 32,
6. Ibid, p. 36.
7. Ibid, pp. 48-9.
8. Ibid, pp. 144-5.
9. Ibid, pp. 146-7.
10. Ibid, p. 147.
11. G. J. Turner, 'Social Class and Children's Language of Control at Age Five and Seven', in Basil Bernstein (ed.), *Class, Codes and Control*, vol. 2: *Applied Studies Towards a Sociology of Language* (London: Routledge & Kegan Paul, 1973) pp. 135-6.
12. George Steiner, 'In Bluebeard's Castle', *Listener*, 15 April 1971.
13. Bernard Rosenberg, 'Mass Culture in America', in Bernard Rosenberg and David Manning White (eds), *Mass Culture: The Popular Arts in America* (New York: Free Press, 1964) p. 5.
14. B. Sugarman, 'Involvement in Youth Culture, Academic Achievement and Conformity in School', *British Journal of Sociology*, June 1967, p. 158.
15. Mary Douglas, 'Do Dogs Laugh?: a Cross-Cultural Approach to Body Symbolism', *Journal of Psychosomatic Research*, 15, 1971, p. 389.
16. M. A. K. Halliday, *Language as Social Semiotic: the Social Interpretation of Language and Meaning* (London: Edward Arnold, 1978) p. 161.
17. Ibid., p. 172.
18. Ibid., p. 180.
19. Dell Hymes, *Foundations in Sociolinguistics: an Ethnographical Approach* (London: Tavistock Publications, 1977) p. 51.
20. Ibid, p. 4.
21. George Melly, *Revolt into Style: the Pop Arts in Britain* (London: Allen Lane, 1970) p. 206.
22. Richard M. Owens and Tony Lane, *American Denim: a New Folk Art* (New York: Abrams, 1975) pp. 38-9.
23. Ibid, p. 38.
24. Marshall McLuhan, *Understanding Media* (London: Routledge, 1964)

p. 231. See also George Steiner, 'The Retreat from the Word', *Listener*, 14
and 21 July 1960.

25. Simon Frith, 'Rock Lyrics', *Listener*, 26 June 1980.
26. Donald Davie, 'British and American English', *Listener*, 23 January 1969.
27. The two vintage 'Dear Bill' letters referring to the Royal Wedding are to be
found in the issues of *Private Eye* for 31 July and 14 August 1981.
28. John Wells, *Anyone for Denis?*

CHAPTER 3: POP MUSIC AS A CULTURAL CARRIER

1. Colin MacInnes, 'Pop Music', *Twentieth Century*, February 1958.
2. George Melly, *Revolt into Style: the Pop Arts in Britain* (London: Allen
Lane, 1970) p. 7.
3. For an interesting analysis of this, see Nik Cohn, *Pop from the Beginning*
(London: Weidenfeld & Nicolson, 1969) pp. 11-12.
4. Tony Palmer, *All You Need is Love: the Story of Popular Music* (London:
Weidenfeld & Nicolson, 1976) p. 159. Palmer was the *Observer's* music
critic from 1966 to 1974.
5. Melly, *Revolt into Style*, p. 29.
6. For a discussion of this, see Melly, *Revolt into Style*, pp. 39-40.
7. Ibid., p. 46.
8. *The Times*, 12 December 1980.
9. Cohn, *Pop from the Beginning*, p. 67.
10. Quoted by Tom Nairn, 'On the subversiveness of Art Students', *Listener*, 17
October 1968. The author had himself been a lecturer in sociology at the
Hornsey School of Art.
11. Adrian Mitchell, 'Beatles', reprinted in *Listener*, 3 October 1968.
12. Quoted in Michael Wale, *Voxpop: Profiles of the Pop Process* (London:
Harrap, 1972) pp. 12-13.
13. The issue of *New Musical Express* for 7 March 1981 had 60 pages and cost
30p.
14. Dick Hebdige, *Subculture: the Meaning of Style* (London: Methuen, 1979)
p. 25.

CHAPTER 4: THE LEXICOGRAPHER'S WATERLOO

1. J. Isaacs, in a radio talk, 'What is a Dictionary?', subsequently printed in
Listener, 7 November 1957.
2. Ibid.
3. Such action is in fact illegal. The definitions in a dictionary are copyright,
as if they were paragraphs in a novel. To avoid all risk of prosecution, every
definition in a dictionary must be brand-new. Even the complete choice of
words in a dictionary is copyright.
4. Samuel Johnson, *Plan of a Dictionary of the English Language* (1747) p. 18.
5. Henry Morley (ed.), *The Earlier Life and the Chief Earlier Works of Daniel
Defoe* (1889) pp. 125-6.

6. Temple Scott (ed.), *The Prose Works of Jonathan Swift, DD* (1907) vol. XI, pp. 14–15.
7. Benjamin Martin, *Lingua Britannica Reformata* (1749).
8. Samuel Johnson, Preface to the *Dictionary* (1755) vol. 1.
9. 'General Explanations', *The Oxford English Dictionary* (1933) vol. 1, p. xxviii.
10. Today they might well have written 'sub-cultures'.
11. 'General Explanations', p. xxvii.
12. Lewis Jones, 'Dictionaries', *Listener*, 26 December 1963.
13. *Melody Maker*, 24 January 1981.
14. Foreword to *Collins English Dictionary* (London and Glasgow: Collins, 1979) p. vii.
15. Ibid., p. vii.

CHAPTER 5: WRONG-FOOTING THE ENEMY

1. *International Times*, 14 October 1966.
2. Letter to *My Guy*, 1 September 1979.
3. Column heading in *Jackie*, 7 May 1966.
4. *Jackie*, 4 February 1968.
5. *Private Eye*, 19 January 1971.
6. *Melody Maker*, 29 May 1979.
7. *Jackie*, 7 February 1981.
8. *Jackie*, 11 January 1964.
9. *Private Eye*, 23 August 1974.
10. Jeff Nuttall, *Bomb Culture* (London: MacGibbon & Kee, 1968).
11. *Private Eye*, 5 June 1970.
12. *Guardian*, 12 March 1979.
13. Letter to *Pink*, 12 May 1979.
14. *Pink*, 12 May 1979.
15. *Jackie*, 18 January 1969.
16. *Jackie*, 24 January 1981.
17. *Daily Mirror*, 22 March 1979.
18. *Jackie*, 9 January 1965.
19. *New Musical Express*, 27 July 1956.
20. *My Guy*, 1 September 1979.
21. *New Musical Express*, 13 January 1956.
22. *Private Eye*, 5 June 1970.
23. Nuttall, *Bomb Culture*.
24. *Foul*, June 1974.
25. Interview with pop group in *Rolling Stone*, 30 November 1978.
26. *Daily Telegraph*, 3 February 1981.
27. *Foul*, June 1974.
28. *Judy Annual for Girls*, 1968 edition (London: D. C. Thomson).
29. *Guardian*, 13 March 1979.
30. *Jackie*, 24 January 1981.
31. *Motor Cycle Weekly*, 31 January 1981.
32. *Judy Annual for Girls*, 1968.
33. *Jackie*, 20 July 1968.

CHAPTER 6: THE INFLUENCE OF REAL AND IMAGINARY BLACKS

1. Dick Hebdige, *Subculture: the Meaning of Style* (London: Methuen, 1979) p. 55.
2. Edward Bone, *The Negro Novel in America* (Yale University Press, 1965) pp. 53-4. This is of great value in understanding black culture in general. Its analysis and insight go deeper and wider than the title of the book indicates.
3. Thomas Kochman (ed.), *Rappin' and Stylin' Out: Communication in Black America* (University of Illinois Press, 1972) p. xi.
4. Kochman, *Rappin' and Stylin' Out*, p. 172. On this, see also J. L. Dillard, *Black English in the United States* (New York: Random House, 1972).
5. A summary of his findings can be found in Kochman, *Rappin' and Stylin' Out*, p. 172 onwards.
6. Colin MacInnes, 'Reggae', *New Society*, 31 December 1970.
7. Quoted in Bone, *The Negro Novel in America*, p. 198. Ellison was born in 1914. His *Invisible Man* won the National Book Award as the best American novel of 1952.
8. *Oz 21*, June 1969.
9. *Attila*, no. 25, 23 October 1971.
10. *Melody Maker*, 27 January 1979.
11. *Black Music*, December 1979.
12. Colin MacInnes, *City of Spades* (London: MacGibbon & Kee, 1957) p. 41.
13. Ibid., p. 47.
14. Hebdige, *Subculture*, p. 45.

CHAPTER 7: YOUTH AND THE LAW

1. Terence Morris, 'The Teenage Criminal', *New Society*, 11 April 1963.
2. Ibid.
3. Ray Gosling, 'The Tough and the Tender', *New Society*, 18 April 1963.
4. Michael Schofield, *Sexual Behaviour of Britain's Teenagers* (London: Central Council of Health Education, 1965).
5. J. and S. Eppels, 'Teenage Values', *New Society*, 14 November, 1963.
6. Advertisement in *New Musical Express*, 18 July 1958.
7. *Sounds*, 1 December 1979.
8. *Gay News*, 23 February 1979.
9. *Spare Rib*, September 1979.
10. *Time Out*, 6 April 1979.
11. Interview with rock group in *Zigzag*, July 1973.
12. *Spare Rib*, January 1979.
13. Letter to *Oz 3*, 1967.
14. *Spare Rib*, April 1975.
15. *International Times*, 14 November 1966.
16. Advertisment in *Sounds*, 3 March 1979.

17. Keith Waterhouse, *Billy Liar* (London: Michael Joseph, 1959).
18. *Gay News*, 23 February 1978.
19. *International Times*, 5 January 1968.
20. *My Guy*, 19 May 1979.
21. *International Times*, 28 November 1966.
22. Pop group, in *New Musical Express*, 6 January 1979.
23. *Oz*, Winter 1973.
24. *Zigzag*, August 1972.
25. *Zigzag*, August 1972.
26. *Oz 18*, February 1969.
27. *Attila*, 16 December 1971.
28. Jamie Mandelkau, *Buttons* (London: Open Gate Books, 1971).
29. *Zigzag*, August 1972.
30. *International Times*, 13 February 1967.

Sources

What follows is not intended to be a comprehensive bibliography of the subject of this book. It refers only to the books and articles which I have found useful during my research. Many others, often with impressive titles and well-known authors, I have found of little value or originality, and I see no point in listing them here.

A. YOUTH CULTURE IN GENERAL

Chapman, Dennis, 'The Autonomous Generation', *Listener*, 17 January 1963.

Coleman, James S., *The Adolescent Society* (New York: Free Press, 1961).

Cross, William, 'Looning about on our Bikes' (London's Hell's Angels), *New Society*, 7 February 1980.

Davies, Bernard, 'Non-Swinging Youth', *New Society*, 3 July 1969.

Eppels, J. and S., 'Teenage Values', *New Society*, 14 and 21 November 1963.

Erikson, Erik H. (ed.), *Youth: Change and Challenge* (New York: Basic Books, 1961).

Forester, Tom, 'The Return of the Mods', *New Society*, 24 May 1979.

Gosling, Ray, *Sum Total* (London: Faber, 1962).

Gosling, Ray, 'The Tough and the Tender' (teenage morals), *New Society*, 18 April 1963.

Hall, Stuart, *et al.*, *Resistance through Rituals* (London: Hutchinson, 1976).

Hebdige, Dick, *Subculture: the Meaning of Style* (London: Methuen, 1979).

Kettle, Martin, 'The Private Worlds of the Drug Taker', *New Society*, 7 February 1980.

Laslett, Peter, 'The Social Revolution of our Time', *Listener*, 11 January 1962.

Laurie, Peter, *Teenage Revolution* (London: Anthony Blond, 1965).

Little, Alan, 'The Young Affluents', *Listener*, 9 May 1963.

Melly, George, *Revolt into Style: the Pop Arts in Britain* (London: Allen Lane, 1970).

Morris, Brian, *An Introduction to Mary Quant's London* (London Museum, 1973).

Morris, Terence, 'The Teenage Criminal', *New Society*, 11 April 1963.

Nairn, Tom, 'On the Subversiveness of Art Students', *Listener*, 17 October 1968.

Nuttall, Jeff, *Bomb Culture* (London: MacGibbon & Kee, 1968).
Owens, Richard M., and Lane, Tony, *American Denim: a New Folk Art* (New York: Abrams, 1975).
Reich, Charles, *The Greening of America* (London: Allen Lane, 1971).
Robins, David, and Cohen, Philip, *Knuckle Sandwich: Growing up in the Working-Class City* (London. Allen Lane, 1978).
Schofield, Michael, *Sexual Behaviour of Britain's Teenagers* (London. Central Council of Health Education, 1965).
Sugarman, B., 'Involvement in Youth Culture, Academic Achievement and Conformity in School', *British Journal of Sociology*, June 1967.
Turner, Graham, 'Ladies will be Ladies', *Sunday Telegraph*, 12 July 1981.
Wilmott, Peter, *Adolescent Boys of East London* (London: Routledge, 1966).

B. POP MUSIC

I cannot pretend that all the reading indicated in sections B, E and F has been wholly pleasurable. If I had not been under such a strong obligation to seek reliable information, I would not willingly have immersed myself in the literature of football, drug-taking, motor-cycling, homosexuality, nihilism and revolution. Nor would I have persevered for very long with files of teenage and student magazines, novels whose attitude to life I found either incomprehensible or loathsome, or music magazines which appeared to me like a never-ending Black Mass, a total prostitution of the God-given possibilities of music. But I can at least now say that I have done it and that the process has been enlightening and, in its way, rewarding.

Cohn, Nik, *Pop from the Beginning* (London: Weidenfeld & Nicolson, 1969).
Eisen, Jonathan (ed.), *The Age of Rock: Sounds of the American Cultural Revolution*, 2 vols (New York: Vintage Books, 1969, 1970).
Frith, Simon, 'Rock Lyrics', *Listener*, 26 June 1980.
MacInnes, Colin, 'Pop Music', *Twentieth Century*, February 1958.
MacInnes, Colin, 'Reggae', *New Society*, 31 December 1970.
Mitchell, Adrian, 'Beatles', *Listener*, 3 October 1968.
Palmer, Tony, *All You Need is Love: the Story of Popular Music* (London: Weidenfeld & Nicolson, 1976).
Wale, Michael, *Voxpop: Profiles of the Pop Process* (London: Harrap, 1972).
Black Music.
Hot Press.
Melody Maker.
New Musical Express.
Rolling Stone.
Sounds.

C. THE BLACK COMMUNITY AND BLACK CULTURE

Bone, Edward, *The Negro Novel in America* (Yale University Press, 1965).
Cashman, Ernest, *Rastaman: the Rastafarian Movement in England* (London: Allen & Unwin, 1979).
Dillard, J. L., *Black English in the United States* (New York: Random House, 1972).
Kochman, Thomas (ed.), *Rappin' and Stylin' Out: Communication in Black America* (University of Illinois Press, 1972).
MacInnes, Colin, *City of Spades* (London: MacGibbon & Kee, 1957).
MacInnes, Colin, *Absolute Beginners* (London: MacGibbon & Kee, 1959).

D. LANGUAGE AND CONTEMPORARY SOCIETY

Bernstein, Basil (ed.), *Class, Codes and Control*, vol. 1: *Theoretical Studies Towards a Sociology of Language* (1971); vol. 2: *Applied Studies Towards a Sociology of Language* (1973); vol. 3: *Towards a Theory of Educational Transmissions* (London: Routledge & Kegan Paul).
Davie, Donald, 'British and American English', *Listener*, 23 January 1969.
Halliday, M. A. K., *Language as Social Semiotic: the Social Interpretation of Language and Meaning* (London: Edward Arnold, 1976).
Hymes, Dell, *Foundations in Sociolinguistics: an Ethnographical Approach* (London: Tavistock Publications, 1977).
Isaacs, J., 'What is a Dictionary?', *Listener*, 7 November 1957.
Jones, Lewis, 'Dictionaries', *Listener*, 26 December 1963.
McLuhan, Marshall, *Understanding Media* (London: Routledge, 1964).
Ross, Alan S. C., with Brackenbury, Robin, 'U and Non-U Today', *New Society*, 22 August 1968.
Steiner, George, 'The Retreat from the Word', *Listener*, 14 and 21 July 1960.
Steiner, George, 'In Bluebeard's Castle', *Listener*, 15 April 1971.

E. MAGAZINES MUCH READ BY TEENAGERS

Foul.
Honey.
Jackie.
Mates.
Motor Cycle Weekly.

My Guy.
Oh Boy!
Pink.
Schoolkids Oz.
Superbike.

F. OTHER MAGAZINES

Attila.
Gay News.
Home Grown.
International Times.
Oz.
New Society

Private Eye.
Spare Rib.
Time Out.
Undercurrents.
Zigzag.

Index